A KISS
FOR CINDERELLA

THE PLAYS OF J. M. BARRIE.

DEAR BRUTUS
QUALITY STREET.
THE ADMIRABLE CRICHTON.
WHAT EVERY WOMAN KNOWS.
ALICE SIT-BY-THE-FIRE.
A KISS FOR CINDERELLA.
OLD LADY SHOWS HER MEDALS, AND OTHER PLAYS.
THE TWELVE-POUND LOOK, AND OTHER PLAYS.

Other Volumes in preparation.

WORKS BY J. M. BARRIE.

A WINDOW IN THRUMS.
AULD LICHT IDYLLS.
MY LADY NICOTINE.
WHEN A MAN'S SINGLE.
MARGARET OGILVY.
THE LITTLE WHITE BIRD.
PETER PAN IN KENSINGTON GARDENS.
With 50 Illustrations by ARTHUR RACKHAM.
PETER AND WENDY.
Illustrated by F. D. BEDFORD.
PETER PAN AND WENDY.
Illustrated by MABEL LUCIE ATTWELL.
THE ADMIRABLE CRICHTON.
Illustrated by HUGH THOMSON.
QUALITY STREET.
Illustrated by HUGH THOMSON.

ECHOES OF THE WAR.
Containing: The Old Lady shows her Medals, The New Word, Barbara's Wedding, A Well-Remembered Voice. In One Volume.
HALF-HOURS.
Containing: Rosalind, Pantaloon, The Will, The Twelve-Pound Look. In One Volume.

COURAGE.
The Rectorial Address to the Students of St. Andrews University.

THE KIRRIEMUIR EDITION OF THE WORKS OF J. M. BARRIE.

In sets of Ten Volumes.

AULD LICHT IDYLLS.
BETTER DEAD.
AN EDINBURGH ELEVEN.
A WINDOW IN THRUMS.
MARGARET OGILVY.
WHEN A MAN'S SINGLE.
MY LADY NICOTINE.
THE LITTLE MINISTER.
THE LITTLE WHITE BIRD.
PETER AND WENDY.
SENTIMENTAL TOMMY.
TOMMY AND GRIZEL.

LONDON: HODDER AND STOUGHTON LTD.

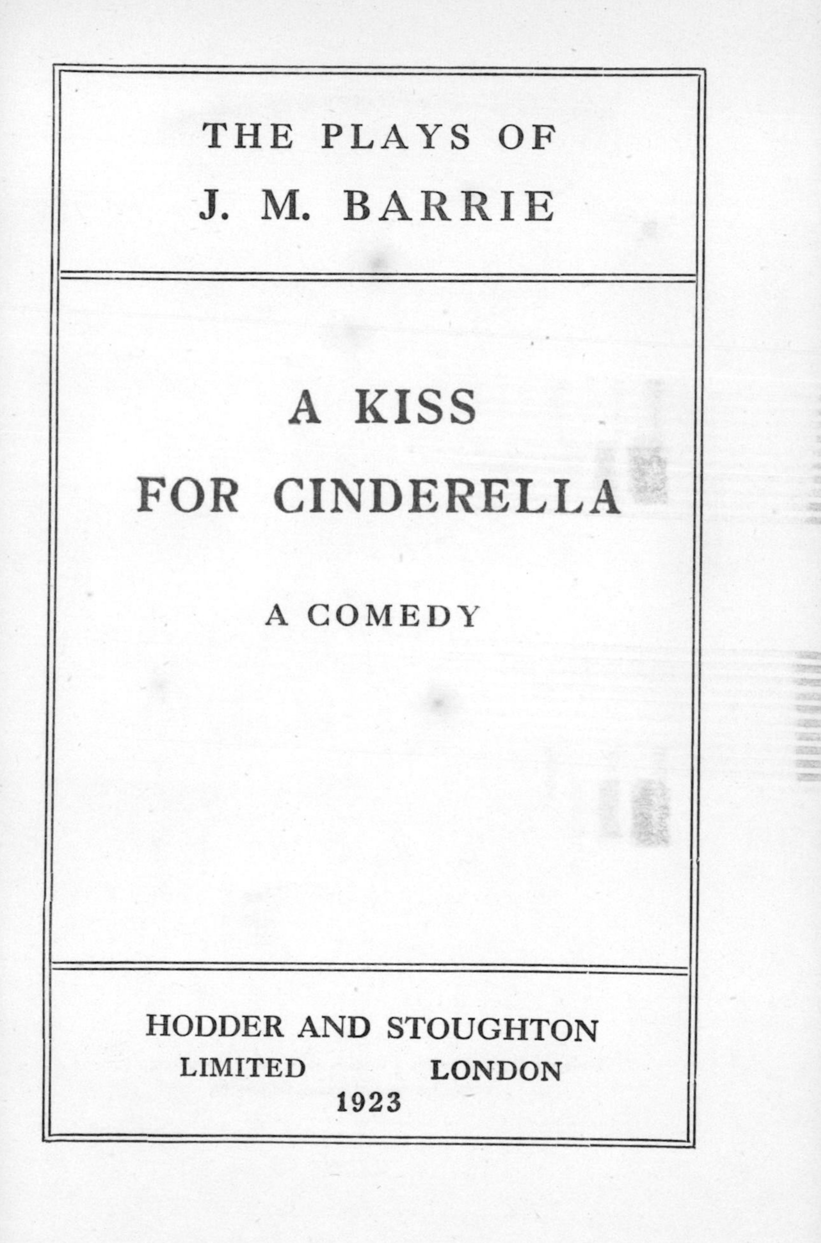

THE PLAYS OF
J. M. BARRIE

A KISS FOR CINDERELLA

A COMEDY

HODDER AND STOUGHTON
LIMITED LONDON
1923

Made and Printed in Great Britain by T. and A. Constable Ltd.
at the University Press, Edinburgh

I

The least distinguished person in 'Who's Who' has escaped, as it were, from that fashionable crush, and is spending a quiet evening at home. He is curled up in his studio, which is so dark that he would be invisible, had we not obligingly placed his wicker chair just where the one dim ray from the stove may strike his face. His eyes are closed luxuriously, and we could not learn much about him without first poking our fingers into them. According to the tome mentioned (to which we must return him before morning), Mr. Bodie is sixty-three, has exhibited in the Royal Academy, and is at present unmarried. They do not proclaim him comparatively obscure: they left it indeed to him to say the final word on this subject, and he has hedged. Let us put it in this way, that he occupies more space in his wicker chair than in the book, where nevertheless he looks as if it was rather lonely not to be a genius. He is a painter for the nicest of reasons, that it is delightful to live and die in a messy studio; for our part, we too should have become a painter had it not been that we always lost our paint-box. There is no spirited bidding to acquire Mr. Bodie's canvases: he loves them at first sight himself, and has often got up in the night to see how they are faring; but ultimately he has turned cold to them, and has even been known to offer them, in lieu of alms, to beggars, who departed cursing. We have a weakness for persons who don't get on, and so cannot help adding, though it is no business of ours, that Mr. Bodie had private means. Curled up in his wicker chair he is rather like an elderly cupid. We wish we could warn him that the policeman is coming.

The policeman comes: in his hand the weapon that has knocked down more malefactors than all the batons—the bull's-eye. He strikes with it now, right and left, revealing, as if she had just entered the room, a replica of the Venus of Milo, taller than himself though he is a stalwart. It is the first meeting of these two, but, though a man who can come to the boil, he is as little moved by her as she by him. After the first glance she continues her reflections. Her smile over his head vaguely displeases him. For two pins he would arrest her.

The lantern finds another object, more worthy of his attention, the artist. Mr. Bodie is more restive under the light than was his goddess, perhaps because he is less accustomed to being stared at. He blinks and sits up.

MR. BODIE (*giving his visitor a lesson in manners*). I beg your pardon, officer.

POLICEMAN (*confounded*). Not that, sir; not at all.

MR. BODIE (*pressing his advantage*). But I insist on begging your pardon, officer.

POLICEMAN. I don't see what for, sir.

MR. BODIE (*fancying himself*). For walking uninvited into the abode of a law-abiding London citizen, with whom I have not the pleasure of being acquainted.

POLICEMAN (*after thinking this out*). But I 'm the one as has done that, sir.

MR. BODIE (*with neat surprise*). So you are, I beg your pardon, officer.

(*With pardonable pride in himself* MR. BODIE *turns on the light. The studio, as we can now gather from its sloped roof, is at the top of a house; and its window is heavily screened, otherwise we might see the searchlights through it, showing that we are in the period of the great war. Though no one speaks of* MR. BODIE'S *pictures as Bodies, which is the true test of fame, he is sufficiently eminent not to have works of art painted or scratched on his walls, mercy has been shown even to the panels of his door, and he is handsomely stingy of draperies. The Venus stands so prominent that the studio is evidently hers rather than his. The stove has been brought forward so that he can rest his feet on it, whichever of his easy chairs he is sitting in, and he also falls over it at times when stepping back to consider his latest failure. On a shelf is a large stuffed penguin, which is to be one of the characters in the play, and on each side of this shelf are two or three tattered magazines. We had hankered after giving* MR. BODIE *many rows of books, but were well aware that he would get only blocks of wood so cleverly painted to look like books that they would deceive every one except the audience. Everything may be real on the stage except the books. So there are only a few magazines in the studio (and very likely when the curtain rings up it will be found that they are painted too). But*

MR. BODIE *was a reader ; he had books in another room, and the careworn actor who plays him must suggest this by his manner.*

Our POLICEMAN *is no bookman ; we who write happen to have it from himself that he had not bought a book since he squeezed through the sixth standard : very tight was his waist that day, he told us, and he had to let out every button. Nevertheless it was literature of a sort that first brought him into our ken. He was our local constable : and common interests, as in the vagaries of the moon, gradually made him and us cease to look at each other askance. We fell into the way of chatting with him and giving him the evening papers we had bought to read as we crossed the streets. One of his duties was to herd the vagrant populace under our arches during air-raids, and at such times he could be properly gruff, yet comforting, like one who would at once run in any bomb that fell in his beat. When he had all his flock nicely plastered against the dank walls he would occasionally come to rest beside us, and thaw, and discuss the newspaper article that had interested him most. It was seldom a war-record; more frequently it was something on the magazine page, such as a symposium by the learned on 'Do you Believe in Love at First Sight?' Though reticent in many matters he would face this problem openly; with the guns cracking all around, he would ask for our views wistfully; he spoke of love without a blush, as something recognised officially at Scotland Yard. At this time he had been in love, to his own knowledge, for several weeks, but whether the god had struck him at first sight he was not certain; he was most anxious to know, and it was in the hope of our being able to help him out that he told us his singular story. On his face at such times was often an amazed look, as if he were staring at her rather than at us, and seeing a creature almost beyond belief. Our greatest success was in saying that perhaps she had fallen in love at first sight with him, which on reflection nearly doubled him up. He insisted on knowing what had made us put forward this extraordinary suggestion; he would indeed scarcely leave our company that night, and discussed the possibility with us very much as if it were a police case.*

Our POLICEMAN'S *romance, now to be told, began, as we begin, with his climbing up into* MR. BODIE'S *studio.* MR. BODIE *having turned on the light gave him the nasty look that means 'And now, my man, what can I do for you?' Our* POLICEMAN, *however, was not one to be worsted without striking a blow. He strode to the door, as he has told us, and pointed to a light in the passage.)*

POLICEMAN (*in his most brow-beating voice, so well known under the arches*). Look here, sir, it 's that.

MR. BODIE. I don't follow.

POLICEMAN. Look at that passage window. (*With natural pride in language.*) You are showing too much illumination.

BODIE. Oh! well, surely—

POLICEMAN (*with professional firmness*). It 's

agin the regulations. A party in the neighbouring skylight complains.

BODIE (*putting out the light*). If that will do for to-night, I 'll have the window boarded up.

POLICEMAN. Anything so long as it obscures the illumination.

BODIE (*irritated*). Shuts out the light.

POLICEMAN (*determinedly*). Obscures the illumination.

BODIE (*on reflection*). I remember now, I did have that window boarded up.

POLICEMAN (*who has himself a pretty vein of sarcasm*). I don't see the boards.

BODIE. Nor do I see the boards. (*Pondering.*) Can she have boned them ?

POLICEMAN. She ? (*He is at once aware that it has become a more difficult case.*)

BODIE. You are right. She is scrupulously honest, and if she took the boards we may be sure that I said she could have them. But that only adds to the mystery.

POLICEMAN (*obligingly*). Mystery ?

BODIE. Why this passion for collecting

boards? Try her with a large board, officer. Extraordinary!

POLICEMAN (*heavily*). I don't know what you are talking about, sir. Are you complaining of some woman?

BODIE. Now that is the question. Am I? As you are here, officer, there is something I want to say to you. But I should dislike getting her into trouble.

POLICEMAN (*stoutly*). No man what is a man wants to get a woman into trouble unnecessary.

BODIE (*much struck*). That 's true! That 's *absolutely* true, officer.

POLICEMAN (*badgered*). It 's true, but there 's nothing remarkable about it.

BODIE. Excuse me.

POLICEMAN. See here, sir, I 'm just an ordinary policeman.

BODIE. I can't let that pass. If I may say so, you have impressed me most deeply. I wonder if I might ask a favour of you. Would you mind taking off your helmet? As it happens, I have never seen a policeman without his helmet.

(*The perplexed officer puts his helmet on the table.*)

Thank you. (*Studying the effect.*) Of course I knew they took off. You sit also?

(*The* POLICEMAN *sits.*)

Very interesting.

POLICEMAN. About this woman, sir—

BODIE. We are coming to her. Perhaps I ought to tell you my name—Mr. Bodie. (*Indicating the Venus.*) This is Mrs. Bodie. No, I am not married. It is merely a name given her because she is my ideal.

POLICEMAN. You gave me a turn.

BODIE. Now that I think of it, I believe the name was given to her by the very woman we are talking about.

POLICEMAN (*producing his note-book*). To begin with, who is the woman we are talking about?

BODIE (*becoming more serious*). On the surface, she is just a little drudge. These studios are looked after by a housekeeper, who employs this girl to do the work.

POLICEMAN. H'm! Sleeps on the premises?

BODIE. No ; she is here from eight to six.

POLICEMAN. Place of abode ?

BODIE. She won't tell any one that.

POLICEMAN. Aha ! What 's the party's name ?

BODIE. Cinderella.

(*The* POLICEMAN *writes it down unmoved.* MR. BODIE *twinkles.*)

Haven't you heard that name before ?

POLICEMAN. Can't say I have, sir. But I 'll make inquiries at the Yard.

BODIE. It was really I who gave her that name, because she seemed such a poor little neglected waif. After the girl in the story-book, you know.

POLICEMAN. No, sir, I don't know. In the Force we find it impossible to keep up with current fiction.

BODIE. She was a girl with a broom. There must have been more in the story than that, but I forget the rest.

POLICEMAN. The point is, that 's not the name she calls herself by.

BODIE. Yes, indeed it is. I think she was

called something else when she came—Miss Thing, or some such name; but she took to the name of Cinderella with avidity, and now she absolutely denies that she ever had any other.

POLICEMAN. Parentage?

BODIE (*now interested in his tale*). That 's another odd thing. I seem to remember vaguely her telling me that her parents when alive were very humble persons indeed. Touch of Scotch about her, I should say—perhaps from some distant ancestor; but Scotch words and phrases still stick to the Cockney child like bits of egg-shell to a chicken.

POLICEMAN (*writing*). Egg-shell to chicken.

BODIE. I find, however, that she has lately been telling the housekeeper quite a different story.

POLICEMAN (*like a counsel*). Proceed.

BODIE. According to this, her people were of considerable position—a Baron and Baroness, in fact.

POLICEMAN. Proceed.

BODIE. The only other relatives she seems

to have mentioned are two sisters of unprepossessing appearance.

POLICEMAN (*cleverly*). If this story is correct, what is she doing here ?

BODIE. I understand there is something about her father having married again, and her being badly treated. She doesn't expect this to last. It seems that she has reason to believe that some very remarkable change may take place in her circumstances at an early date, at a ball for which her godmother is to get her what she calls an invite. This is evidently to be a very swagger function at which something momentous is to occur, the culminating moment being at midnight.

POLICEMAN (*writing*). Godmother. Invite. Twelve P.M. Fishy ! Tell me about them boards now.

BODIE (*who is evidently fond of the child*). You can't think how wistful she is to get hold of boards. She has them on the brain. Carries them off herself into the unknown.

POLICEMAN. I dare say she breaks them up for firewood.

BODIE. No; she makes them into large boxes.

POLICEMAN (*sagaciously*). Very likely to keep things in.

BODIE. She has admitted that she keeps things in them. But what things? Ask her that, and her mouth shuts like a trap.

POLICEMAN. Any suspicions?

(MR. BODIE *hesitates. It seems absurd to suspect this waif—and yet!*)

BODIE. I'm sorry to say I have. I don't know what the things are, but I do know they are connected in some way with Germany.

POLICEMAN (*darkly*). Proceed.

BODIE (*really troubled*). Officer, she is too curious about Germany.

POLICEMAN. That's bad.

BODIE. She plies me with questions about it —not openly—very cunningly.

POLICEMAN. Such as—?

BODIE. For instance, what would be the punishment for an English person caught hiding aliens in this country?

POLICEMAN. If she's up to games of that kind—

BODIE. Does that shed any light on the boxes, do you think?

POLICEMAN. She can't keep them shut up in boxes.

BODIE. I don't know. She is extraordinarily dogged. She knows a number of German words.

POLICEMAN. That 's ugly.

BODIE. She asked me lately how one could send a letter to Germany without Lord Haig knowing. By the way, do you, by any chance, know anything against a firm of dressmakers called *Celeste et Cie*?

POLICEMAN. Celest A. C.? No, but it has a German sound.

BODIE. It 's French.

POLICEMAN. Might be a blind.

BODIE. I think she lives at Celeste's. Now I looked up Celeste et Cie in the telephone book, and I find they are in Bond Street. Immensely fashionable.

POLICEMAN. She lives in Bond Street? London 's full of romance, sir, to them as knows where to look for it—namely, the police. Is she on the premises?

BODIE (*reluctantly*). Sure to be; it isn't six yet.

POLICEMAN (*in his most terrible voice*). Well, leave her to me.

BODIE. You mustn't frighten her. I can't help liking her. She 's so extraordinarily *homely* that you can't be with her many minutes before you begin thinking of your early days. Where were you born, officer ?

POLICEMAN. I 'm from Badgery.

BODIE. She 'll make you think of Badgery.

POLICEMAN (*frowning*). She had best try no games on me.

BODIE. She will have difficulty in answering questions ; she is so used to asking them. I never knew a child with such an appetite for information. She doesn't search for it in books ; indeed the only book of mine I can remember ever seeing her read, was a volume of fairy tales.

POLICEMAN (*stupidly*). Well, that don't help us much. What kind of questions ?

BODIE. Every kind. What is the Censor ? Who is Lord *Times* ?—she has heard people here talking of that paper and its proprietor, and has mixed them up in the quaintest way ; then again

—when a tailor measures a gentleman's legs what does he mean when he says—26, 4—32, 11 ? What are doctors up to when they tell you to say 99 ? In finance she has an almost morbid interest in the penny.

POLICEMAN. The penny ? It 's plain the first thing to find out is whether she 's the slavey she seems to be, or a swell in disguise.

BODIE. You won't find it so easy.

POLICEMAN. Excuse me, sir ; we have an infall*ay*ble way at Scotland Yard of finding out whether a woman is common or a lady.

BODIE (*irritated*). An infallible way.

POLICEMAN (*firmly*). Infallayble.

BODIE. I should like to know what it is.

POLICEMAN. There is nothing against my telling you. (*He settles down to a masterly cross-examination.*) Where, sir, does a common female keep her valuables when she carries them about on her person ?

BODIE. In her pocket, I suppose.

POLICEMAN. And you suppose correctly. But where does a lady keep them ?

BODIE. In the same place, I suppose.

POLICEMAN. There you suppose wrongly. No, sir, here. (*He taps his own chest, and indicates discreetly how a lady may pop something down out of sight.*)

BODIE (*impressed*). I believe you are right, officer.

POLICEMAN. I am right—it 's infallayble. A lady, what with drink and suchlike misfortunes, may forget all her other refinements, but she never forgets that. At the Yard it 's considered as sure as finger-marks.

BODIE. Strange! I wonder who was the first woman to do it. It couldn't have been Eve this time, officer.

POLICEMAN (*after reflecting*). I see your point. And now I want just to have a look at the party unbeknownst to her. Where could I conceal myself?

BODIE. Hide?

POLICEMAN. Conceal myself.

BODIE. That small door opens on to my pantry, where she washes up.

POLICEMAN (*peeping in*). It will do. Now bring her up.

BODIE. It doesn't seem fair—I really can't—

POLICEMAN. War-time, sir.

(MR. BODIE *decides that it is patriotic to ring. The* POLICEMAN *emerges from the pantry with a slavey's hat and jacket.*)

These belong to the party, sir?

BODIE. I forgot. She keeps them in there. (*He surveys the articles with some emotion.*) Gaudy feathers. And yet that hat may have done some gallant things. The brave apparel of the very poor! Who knows, officer, that you and I are not at this moment on rather holy ground.

POLICEMAN (*stoutly*). I see nothing wrong with the feathers. I must say, sir, I like the feathers.

(*He slips into the pantry with the hat and jacket, but forgets his helmet, over which the artist hastily jams a flower bowl. There were visiting-cards in the bowl and they are scattered on the floor.* MR. BODIE *sees them not: it is his first attempt at the conspirator, and he sits guiltily with a cigarette just in time to deceive* CINDERELLA, *who charges into the room as from a catapult. This is her usual mode of entrance, and is owing to her desire to give satisfaction.*

Our POLICEMAN, *as he has told us under the arches, was watching her through the keyhole, but his first impressions have been so coloured by subsequent events that it is questionable whether they would be accepted in any court of law. Is prepared to depose that, to the best of his recollection, they were unfavourable. Does not imply by unfavourable any aspersion on her personal appearance. Would accept the phrase 'far from striking' as summing up her first appearance. Would no longer accept the phrase. Had put her down as being a grown woman, but not sufficiently grown. Thought her hair looked to be run up her finger. Did not like this way of doing the hair. Could not honestly say that she seemed even then to be an ordinary slavey of the areas. She was dressed as one, but was suspiciously clean. On the other hand, she had the genuine hungry look. Among more disquieting features noticed a sort of refinement in her voice and manner, which was characteristic of the criminal classes. Knew now that this was caused by the reading of fairy tales and the thinking of noble thoughts. Noted speedily that she was a domineering character who talked sixteen to the dozen, and at such times reminded him of funny old ladies. Was much struck by her eyes, which seemed to suggest that she was all burning inside. This impression was strengthened later when he touched her hands. Felt at once the curious 'homeliness' of her, as commented on by* MR. BODIE, *but could swear on oath that this had not at once made him think of Badgery. Could recall not the slightest symptoms of love at first sight. On the contrary, listened carefully to the conversation between her and* MR. BODIE *and formed a stern conclusion about her. Believed that this was all he could say about his first impression.)*

CINDERELLA (*breathlessly*). Did you rang, sir?

BODIE (*ashamed*). Did I? I did—but—I—I don't know why. If you 're a good servant, you ought to know why.

(*The cigarette, disgusted with him, falls from his mouth; and his little servant flings up her hands to heaven.*)

CINDERELLA (*taking possession of him*). There you go again! Fifty years have you been at it, and you can't hold a seegarette in your mouth *yet*! (*She sternly produces the turpentine.*)

BODIE (*in sudden alarm*). I won't be brushed. I will not be scraped.

CINDERELLA (*twisting him round*). Just look at that tobaccy ash! And I cleaned you up so pretty before luncheon.

BODIE. I will *not* be cleaned again.

CINDERELLA (*in her element*). Keep still.

(*She brushes, scrapes, and turpentines him. In the glory of this she tosses her head at the Venus.*)

I gave Mrs. Bodie a good wipe down this morning with soap and water.

BODIE (*indignant*). That is a little too much. You know quite well I allow no one to touch her.

(CINDERELLA *leaves him and gazes in irritation at the statue.*)

CINDERELLA. What *is* it about the woman ?

BODIE (*in his heat forgetting the* POLICEMAN). She is the glory of glories.

CINDERELLA (*who would be willowy if she were long enough*). She 's thick.

BODIE. Her measurements are perfection. All women long to be like her, but none ever can be.

CINDERELLA (*insisting*). I suppose that 's the reason she has that snigger on her face.

BODIE. That is perhaps the smile of motherhood. Some people think there was once a baby in her arms.

CINDERELLA (*with a new interest in Venus*). Her own ?

BODIE. I suppose so.

CINDERELLA. A married woman then ?

BODIE (*nonplussed*). Don't ask trivial questions.

CINDERELLA (*generously*). It was clever of you to make her.

BODIE. I didn't make her. I was—forestalled. Some other artist chappie did it. (*He likes his little maid again.*) She was dug up, Cinderella, after lying hidden in the ground for more than a thousand years.

CINDERELLA. And the baby gone?

BODIE (*snapping*). Yes.

CINDERELLA. If I had lost my baby I wouldn't have been found with that pleased look on my face, not in a thousand years.

BODIE. Her arms were broken, you see, so she had to drop the baby—

CINDERELLA. She could have up with her knee and catched it—

BODIE (*excitedly*). By heavens, that may just be what she is doing. (*He contemplates a letter to the* 'Times.')

CINDERELLA (*little aware that she may have solved the question of the ages.*) Beauty 's a grand thing.

BODIE. It is.

CINDERELLA. I warrant *she* led them a pretty dance in her day.

BODIE. Men?

CINDERELLA. Umpha! (*Wistfully.*) It must

be fine to have men so mad about you that they go off their feed and roar. (*She turns with a sigh to the dusting of the penguin.*) What did you say this is ?

BODIE (*ignorant of what he is letting himself in for*). A bishop.

CINDERELLA (*nearly choking*). The sort that marries swell couples ?

BODIE. Yes.

CINDERELLA (*huskily, as if it made all the difference to her*). I never thought of that.

BODIE (*kindly*). Why should you, you queer little waif. Do you know why I call you Cinderella ?

CINDERELLA. Fine, I know.

BODIE. Why is it ?

CINDERELLA (*with shy happiness*). It 's because I have such pretty feet.

BODIE. You dear little innocent. (*He thinks shame of his suspicions. He is planning how to get rid of the man in the pantry when she brings him back to hard facts with a bump.*)

CINDERELLA (*in a whisper*). Mr. Bodie, if you wanted to get into Buckingham Palace on the dodge, how would you slip by the policeman? (*She wrings her hands.*) The police is everywhere in war-time.

BODIE (*conscious how near one of them is*). They are—be careful, Cinderella.

CINDERELLA. I am—oh, I am! If you knew the precautions I 'm taking—

BODIE (*miserable*). Sh!

CINDERELLA (*now in a quiver*). Mr. Bodie, you haven't by any chance got an invite for to-night, have you?

BODIE. What for?

CINDERELLA (*as still as the Venus*). For—for a ball.

BODIE. There are no balls in war-time.

CINDERELLA (*dogged*). Just the one. Mr. Bodie, did you ever see the King?

BODIE. The King? Several times.

CINDERELLA (*as white as the Venus*). Was the Prince of Wales with him?

BODIE. Once.

CINDERELLA. What 's he like?

BODIE. Splendid! Quite young, you know. He 's not married.

CINDERELLA (*with awful intensity*). No, not yet.

BODIE. I suppose he is very difficult to satisfy.

CINDERELLA (*knitting her lips*). He has never seen the feet that pleased him.

BODIE. Cinderella, your pulse is galloping. You frighten me. What possesses you?

CINDERELLA (*after hesitating*). There is something I want to tell you. Maybe I 'll not be coming back after to-night. She has paid me up to to-night.

BODIE. Is she sending you away?

CINDERELLA. No. I 've sort of given notice.

BODIE (*disappointed*). You 've got another place?

(*She shuts her mouth like a box.*)

Has it anything to do with the Godmother business?

(*Her mouth remains closed. He barks at her.*)

Don't then. (*He reconsiders her.*) I like you, you know.

CINDERELLA (*gleaming*). It 's fine to be liked.

BODIE. Have you a lonely life?

CINDERELLA. It 's kind of lonely.

BODIE. You won't tell me about your home?

(*She shakes her head.*)

Is there any nice person to look after you in the sort of way in which you look after me?

CINDERELLA. I 'm all alone. There 's just me and my feet.

BODIE. If you go I 'll miss you. We 've had some good times here, Cinderella, haven't we?

CINDERELLA (*rapturously*). We have! You mind that chop you gave me? Hey, hey, hey! (*Considering it judicially.*) That was the most charming chop I ever saw. And many is the lick of soup you 've given me when you thought I looked down-like. Do you mind the chicken that was too high for you? You give me the whole chicken. That was a day.

BODIE. I never meant you to eat it.

CINDERELLA. I didn't eat it all myself. I shared it with them.

BODIE (*inquisitively*). With them? With whom?

(*Her mouth shuts promptly, and he sulks.*

She picks up the visiting-cards that litter the floor.)

CINDERELLA. What a spill! If you 're not messing you 're spilling. Where 's the bowl?

(*She lifts the bowl and discovers the helmet. She is appalled.*)

BODIE (*in an agony of remorse pointing to the door*). Cinderella, quick!

(*But our* POLICEMAN *has emerged and barred the way*).

POLICEMAN (*indicating that it is* MR. BODIE *who must go*). If *you* please, sir.

BODIE. I won't! Don't you dare to frighten her.

POLICEMAN (*settling the matter with the palm of his hand*). That will do. If I need you I 'll call you.

BODIE (*flinching*). Cinderella, it 's —it 's just a form. I won't be far away.

(*He departs reluctantly.*)

POLICEMAN (*sternly*). Stand up.

CINDERELLA (*a quaking figure, who has never sat down*). I 'm standing up.

POLICEMAN. Now, no sauce.

cautious. How do you spend your evenings after you leave this building ?

(Her mouth shuts.)

Have you another and secret occupation ?

(She blanches.)

Has it to do with boxes ? What do you keep in those boxes ? Where is it that these goings-on is going on ? If you won't tell me, I 'm willing to tell you. It 's at A. C. Celest's . . . In Bond Street, W.

(He has levelled his finger at her, but it is a pistol that does not go off. To his chagrin she looks relieved. He tries hammer blows.)

Are you living in guilty splendour ? How do you come to know German words ? How many German words do you think *I* know ? Just one, *espionage.* What 's the German for ' six months hard ' ?

(She is now crumpled, and here he would do well to pause and stride up and down the room. But he cannot leave well alone.)

What 's this nonsense about your feet ?

CINDERELLA (*plucking up courage*). It 's not nonsense.

POLICEMAN. I see nothing particular about your feet.

CINDERELLA. Then I 'm sorry for you.

POLICEMAN. What is it?

CINDERELLA (*softly as if it were a line from the Bible*). Their exquisite smallness and perfect shape.

POLICEMAN (*with a friendly glance at the Venus*). For my part I 'm partial to big women with their noses in the air.

CINDERELLA (*stung*). So is everybody. (*Pathetically.*) I 've tried. But it 's none so easy, with never no butcher's meat in the house. You 'll see where the su-perb shoulders and the haughty manners come from if you look in shop windows and see the whole of a cow turned inside out and 'Delicious' printed on it.

POLICEMAN (*always just*). There 's something in that.

CINDERELLA (*swelling*). But it doesn't matter how fine the rest of you is if you doesn't have small feet.

POLICEMAN. I never give feet a thought.

CINDERELLA. The swells think of nothing else. (*Exploding.*) Wait till you are at the Ball. Many a haughty beauty with superb uppers will come sailing in—as sure of the prize as if 'Delicious' was pinned on her—and then forward steps the Lord Mayor, and, *utterly disregarding her uppers*, he points to the bottom of her skirt, and he says 'Lift!' and she *has* to lift, and there 's a dead silence, and nothing to be heard except the Prince crying 'Throw her out!'

POLICEMAN (*somewhat staggered by her knowledge of the high life*). What 's all this about a ball?

(CINDERELLA *sees she has said too much and her mouth shuts.*)

Was you ever at a ball?

CINDERELLA (*with dignity*). At any rate I've been at the Horse Show.

POLICEMAN. A ball 's not like a Horse Show.

CINDERELLA. You 'll see.

POLICEMAN (*reverting to business*). It all comes to this, are you genteel, or common clay?

CINDERELLA (*pertly*). I leaves that to you.

POLICEMAN. You couldn't leave it in safer hands. I want a witness to this.

CINDERELLA (*startled*). A witness! What are you to do?

(*With terrible self-confidence he has already opened the door and beckoned.* MR. BODIE *comes in anxiously.*)

POLICEMAN. Take note, sir. (*With the affable manner of a conjurer.*) We are now about to try a little experiment, the object being to discover whether this party is genteel or common clay.

CINDERELLA. Oh, Mr. Bodie, what is it?

BODIE (*remembering what he has been told of the Scotland Yard test*). I don't like . . . I won't have it.

POLICEMAN. It gives her the chance of proving once and for all whether she 's of gentle blood.

CINDERELLA (*eagerly*). Does it?

BODIE. I must forbid . . .

CINDERELLA (*with dreadful resolution*). I 'm ready. I wants to know myself.

POLICEMAN. *Ve*—ry well. Now then, I heard

you say that the old party downstairs had paid you your wages to-day.

CINDERELLA. I see nothing you can prove by that. It was a half-week's wages—1s. 7d. Of course I could see my way clearer if it had been 1s. 9d.

POLICEMAN. That 's neither here nor there. We 'll proceed. Now, very likely you wrapped the money up in a screw of paper. Did you ?

(*She is afraid of giving herself away.*)

Thinking won't help you.

CINDERELLA. It 's *my* money.

BODIE. Nobody wants your money, Cinderella.

POLICEMAN. Answer me. Did you ?

CINDERELLA. Yes.

POLICEMAN. Say 'I did.'

CINDERELLA. I did.

POLICEMAN. And possibly for the sake of greater security you tied a string round it—did you ?

CINDERELLA. I did.

POLICEMAN (*after a glance at* MR. BODIE *to indicate that the supreme moment has come*). You then deposited the little parcel—where ?

BODIE (*in an agony*). Cinderella, be careful!

(*She is so dreading to do the wrong thing that she can only stare. Finally, alas, she produces the fatal packet from her pocket. Quiet triumph of our* POLICEMAN.)

BODIE. My poor child!

CINDERELLA (*not realising yet that she has given herself away*). What is it? Go on.

POLICEMAN. That 'll do. You can stand down.

CINDERELLA. You 've found out?

POLICEMAN. I have.

CINDERELLA (*breathless*). And what am I?

POLICEMAN (*kindly*). I 'm sorry.

CINDERELLA. Am I—common clay?

(*They look considerately at the floor; she bursts into tears and runs into the pantry, shutting the door.*)

POLICEMAN (*with melancholy satisfaction*). It 's infall*ay*ble.

BODIE. At any rate it shows that there 's nothing against her.

POLICEMAN (*taking him further from the pantry door, in a low voice*). I dunno. There 's some queer things. Where does she go when she leaves this house? What about that ball?—and her German connection?—and them boards she makes into boxes—and A. C. Celest? Well, I 'll find out.

BODIE (*miserably*). What are you going to do?

POLICEMAN. To track her when she leaves here. I may have to adopt a disguise. I 'm a masterpiece at that.

BODIE. Yes, but—

POLICEMAN (*stamping about the floor with the exaggerated tread of the Law*). I 'll tell you the rest outside. I must make her think that my suspicions are—allayed. (*He goes cunningly to the pantry door and speaks in a loud voice.*) Well, sir, that satisfies me that she 's not the party I was in search of, and so, with your permission, I 'll bid you good evening. What, you 're going out yourself? Then I 'll be very happy to walk part of the way with you.

(*Nodding and winking, he goes off with heavy steps, taking with him the reluctant* MR. BODIE, *who like one mesmerised also departs stamping.*

MISS THING *peeps out to make sure that they are gone. She is wearing her hat and jacket, which have restored her self-respect. The tears have been disposed of with a lick of the palm. She is again a valiant soul who has had too many brushes with the police not to be able to face another with a tight lip. She is going, but she is not going without her wooden board; law or no law she cannot do without wooden boards. She gets it from a corner where it has been artfully concealed. An imprudent glance at the Venus again dispirits her. With a tape she takes the Beauty's measurements and then her own, with depressing results. The Gods at last pity her, and advise an examination of her rival's foot. Excursions, alarms, transport. She compares feet and is glorified. She slips off her shoe and challenges Venus to put it on. Then, with a derisive waggle of her foot at the shamed goddess, the little enigma departs on her suspicious business, little witting that a masterpiece of a constable is on her track.)*

II

It is later in the evening of the same day, and this is such a street as harbours London's poor. The windows are so close to us that we could tap on the only one which shows a light. It is on the ground floor, and makes a gallant attempt to shroud this light with articles of apparel suspended within. Seen as shadows through the blind, these are somehow very like Miss Thing, and almost suggest that she has been hanging herself in several places in one of her bouts of energy. The street is in darkness, save for the meagre glow from a street lamp, whose glass is painted red in obedience to war regulations. It is winter time, and there is a sprinkling of snow on the ground.

Our policeman appears in the street, not perhaps for the first time this evening, and flashes his lantern on the suspect's window, whose signboard (boards again!) we now see bears this odd device,

Celeste et Cie.

The Penny Friend.

Not perhaps for the first time this evening he scratches his head at it. Then he pounds off in pursuit of some client who has just emerged with a pennyworth. We may imagine the two of them in conversation in the next street, the law putting leading questions. Meanwhile the 'fourth' wall of the establishment of Celeste dissolves, but otherwise the street is as it was, and we are now in the position of privileged persons looking in at her window. It is a tiny room in which you could just swing a cat, and here Cinderella swings cats all and every evening. The chief pieces of furniture are a table and a bench, both of which have a suspicious appearance of having been made out of boards by some handy character. There is a penny in the slot fireplace which has evidently been lately fed, there is a piece of carpet that has been beaten into nothingness, but is still a carpet, there is a hearth-rug of brilliant rags that is probably gratified when your toes catch in it and you are hurled against the wall. Two pictures—one of them partly framed—strike a patriotic note, but they may be there purposely to deceive. The room is lit by a lamp, and at first sight presents no sinister aspect unless it comes from four boxes nailed against the walls some five or six feet from the floor. In appearance they are not dissimilar to large grocery boxes, but it is disquieting to note that one of them has been mended with the board we saw lately in Mr. Bodie's studio. When our policeman comes, as come we may be sure he will, the test of his acumen will be his box action.

The persons in the room at present have either no acumen or are familiar with the boxes. There are four of them, besides Cinderella, whom we catch in the act of adding to her means of livelihood. Celeste et Cie, a name that has caught her delicate fancy while she dashed through fashionable quarters, is the Penny Friend because here everything is dispensed for that romantic coin. It is evident that the fame of the emporium has spread. Three would-be customers sit on the bench awaiting their turn listlessly and as genteelly unconscious of each other as society in a dentist's dining-room, while in the centre is Cinderella fitting an elderly gentleman with a new coat. There are pins in her mouth and white threads in the coat, suggesting that this is not her first struggle with it, and one of the difficulties with which she has to contend is that it has already evidently been the coat of a larger man. Cinderella is far too astute a performer to let it be seen that she has difficulties, however. She twists and twirls her patron with careless aptitude, kneads him if need be, and has him in a condition of pulp while she mutters for her own encouragement and his in-

timidation the cryptic remarks employed by tailors, as to the exact meaning of which she has already probed Mr. Bodie.

CINDERELLA (*wandering over her client with a tape*). 35—14. (*She consults a paper on the table.*) Yes, it 's 35—14.

(*She pulls him out, contracts him and takes his elbows measure.*)

28—7 ; 41—12 ; 15—19. (*There is something wrong, and she has to justify her handiwork.*) You was longer when you came on Monday.

GENTLEMAN (*very moved by the importance of the occasion*). Don't be saying that, Missy.

CINDERELLA (*pinning up the tails of his coat*). Keep still.

GENTLEMAN (*with unexpected spirit*). I warns you, Missy, I won't have it cut.

CINDERELLA (*an artist*). I 'll give you the bits.

GENTLEMAN. I prefers to wear them.

(*She compares the coat with the picture of an elegant dummy.*)

Were you going to make me like that picture ?

CINDERELLA. I had just set my heart on copying this one. It 's the Volupty.

GENTLEMAN (*faint-hearted*). I 'm thinkin' I couldn't stand like that man.

CINDERELLA (*eagerly*). Fine you could—with just a little practice. I 'll let you see the effect.

(*She bends one of his knees, extends an arm and curves the other till he looks like a graceful teapot. She puts his stick in one hand and his hat in the other, and he is now coquettishly saluting a lady.*)

GENTLEMAN (*carried away as he looks at himself in a glass*). By Gosh! Cut away, Missy!

CINDERELLA. I 'll need one more try-on. (*Suddenly.*) That 's to say if I 'm here.

GENTLEMAN (*little understanding the poignancy of the remark*). If it would be convenient to you to have the penny now—

CINDERELLA. No, not till I 've earned it. It 's my rule. Good night to you, Mr. Jennings.

GENTLEMAN. Good night, Missy.

(*We see him go out by the door and disappear up the street.*)

CINDERELLA (*sharply*). Next.

(*An old woman comes to the table and* CINDERELLA *politely pretends not to have seen her sitting there.*)

It 's Mrs. Maloney !

MRS. M. Cinders, I have a pain. It 's like a jag of a needle down my side.

CINDERELLA (*with a sinking, for she is secretly afraid of medical cases*). Wait till I pop the therm-mo-mometer in. It 's a real one. (*She says this with legitimate pride. She removes the instrument from* MRS. MALONEY'S *mouth after a prudent interval, and is not certain what to do next.*)

Take a deep breath. . . . Again. . . . Say 99. (*Her ear is against the patient's chest.*)

MRS. M. 99.

CINDERELLA (*at a venture*). Oho !

MRS. M. It ain't there the pain is—it 's down my side.

CINDERELLA (*firmly*). We never say 99 down there.

MRS. M. What 's wrong wi' me ?

CINDERELLA (*candidly*). I don't want for to pretend, Mrs. Maloney, that the 99 is any guidance to me. I can *not* find out what it 's for. I would make so bold as to call your complaint muscular rheumatics if the pain came when you coughed. But you have no cough.

MRS. M. (*coming to close quarters*). No, but he has—my old man. It 's him that has the pains, not me.

CINDERELLA (*hurt*). What for did you pretend it was you?

MRS. M. That was his idea. He was feared you might stop his smoking.

CINDERELLA. And so I will.

MRS. M. What 's the treatment?

CINDERELLA (*writing after consideration on a piece of paper*). One of them mustard leaves.

MRS. M. (*taking the paper*). Is there no medicine?

CINDERELLA (*faltering*). I 'm a little feared about medicine, Mrs. Maloney.

MRS. M. He 'll be a kind of low-spirited if there 's not a lick of medicine.

CINDERELLA. Have you any in the house?

MRS. M. There 's what was left over of the powders my lodger had when the kettle fell on his foot.

CINDERELLA. You could give him one of them when the cough is troublesome. Good night, Mrs. Maloney.

MRS. M. Thank you kindly. (*She puts a penny on the table.*)

CINDERELLA (*with polite surprise*). What 's that ?

MRS. M. It 's the penny.

CINDERELLA. So it is ! Good night, Mrs. Maloney.

MRS. M. Good night, Cinders.

(*She departs. The penny falls into* CINDERELLA'S *box with a pleasant clink.*)

CINDERELLA. Next.

(*A woman of 35 comes forward. She is dejected, thin-lipped, and unlovable.*)

MARION (*tossing her head*). You 're surprised to see *me*, I dare say.

CINDERELLA (*guardedly*). I haven't the pleasure of knowing you.

MARION (*glancing at the remaining occupant of the bench*). Is that man sleeping ? Who is he ? I don't know him.

CINDERELLA. He 's sleeping. What can I do for you?

MARION (*harshly*). Nothing, I dare say. I 'm at Catullo's Buildings. Now they 're turning me out. They say I 'm not respectable.

CINDERELLA (*enlightened*). You 're — that woman?

MARION (*defiantly*). That 's me.

CINDERELLA (*shrinking*). I don't think there 's nothing I could do for you.

MARION (*rather appealing*). Maybe there is. I see you 've heard my story. They say there 's a man comes to see me at times though he has a wife in Hoxton.

CINDERELLA. I 've heard.

MARION. So I 'm being turned out.

CINDERELLA. I don't think it 's a case for me.

MARION. Yes, it is.

CINDERELLA. Are you terrible fond of him?

MARION. Fond of him! Damn him!

(CINDERELLA *shrinks.* MARION *makes sure that the man is asleep.*)

Cinders, they 've got the story wrong; it 's me as is his wife; I was married to him in a church. He met that woman long after and took up with her.

CINDERELLA. What! Then why do you not tell the truth?

MARION. It 's my pride keeps me from telling. I would rather be thought to be the wrong 'un he likes than the wife the law makes him help.

CINDERELLA. Is that pride?

MARION. It 's all the pride that 's left to me.

CINDERELLA. I 'm awful sorry for you, but I can't think of no advice to give you.

MARION. It 's not advice I want.

CINDERELLA. What is it then?

MARION. It 's pity. I fling back all the gutter words they fling at me, but my heart, Cinders, is wet at times. It 's wet for one to pity me.

CINDERELLA. I pity you.

MARION. You 'll tell nobody?

CINDERELLA. No.

MARION. Can I come in now and again at a time?

CINDERELLA. I 'll be glad to see you—if I 'm here.

MARION. I 'll be slipping away now; he 's waking up. (*She puts down her penny.*)

CINDERELLA. I 'm not doing it for no penny.

MARION. You 've got to take it. That 's my pride. But—I wish you well, Cinders.

CINDERELLA. I like you. I wish you would wish me luck. Say 'Good luck to you to-night, Cinderella.'

MARION. Why to-night?

(*The little waif, so practical until now, is afire inside again. She needs a confidant almost as much as* MARION.)

CINDERELLA (*hastily*). You see—

(*The* MAN *sits up.*)

Good evening, Missis.

MARION. Good luck to you to-night, Cinderella.

(*She goes.*)

(*The* MAN *slips forward and lifts the penny.*)

CINDERELLA (*returning to earth sharply*). Put that down.

MAN. I was only looking at the newness of it. I was just admiring the design.

(*The newness and the design both disappear into the box. A bearded person wearing the overalls of a seafaring man lurches down the street and enters the emporium. Have we seen him before? Who can this hairy monster be?*)

POLICEMAN (*in an incredibly gruff voice*). I want a pennyworth.

CINDERELLA (*unsuspecting*). Sit down. (*She surveys the coster.*) It 's you that belongs to the shirt, isn't it?

MAN. Yes; is 't ready?

CINDERELLA. It 's ready.

(*It proves to be not a shirt, but a 'front' of linen, very stiff and starched. The laundress cautiously retains possession of it.*)

The charge is a penny.

MAN. On delivery.

CINDERELLA. Before delivery.

MAN. Surely you can trust me.

CINDERELLA. You 've tried that on before, my man. Never again! All in this street knows my rule,—Trust in the Lord—every other person, cash.

(*A penny and a 'shirt' pass between them and he departs.*

CINDERELLA *turns her attention to the newcomer.*)

What 's your pleasure ?

POLICEMAN. Shave, please.

CINDERELLA (*quivering before his beard*). Shave ! I shaves in an ordinary way, but I don't know as I could tackle that.

POLICEMAN. I thought you was a barber.

CINDERELLA (*stung*). I 'll get the lather.

(*She goes doubtfully into what she calls her bedroom.*

He seizes this opportunity to survey the room. A remarkable man this, his attention is at once riveted on the boxes, but before he can step on a chair and take a peep the barber returns with the implements of her calling. He reaches his chair in time not to be caught by her. She brings a bowl of soap and water and a towel, which she puts round him in the correct manner.)

CINDERELLA. You 're thin on the top.

POLICEMAN (*in his winding sheet*). I 've all run to beard.

CINDERELLA (*the ever ready*). I have a ointment for the hair; it is my own invention. The price is a penny.

POLICEMAN (*gruffly*). Beard, please.

CINDERELLA. I 've got some voice drops.

POLICEMAN. Beard, please.

CINDERELLA (*as she prepares the lather*). Is the streets quiet ?

POLICEMAN (*cunningly*). Hereabouts they are; but there 's great doings in the fashionable quarters. A ball, I 'm told.

CINDERELLA (*gasping*). You didn't see no peculiar person about in this street ?

POLICEMAN. How peculiar ?

CINDERELLA. Like a—a flunkey ?

POLICEMAN. Did I now—or did I not ?

CINDERELLA (*eagerly*). He would be carrying an invite maybe; it 's a big card.

POLICEMAN. I can't say I saw him.

(*Here an astonishing thing happens. The head of a child rises from one of the boxes. She is unseen by either of the mortals.*)

CINDERELLA (*considering the beard*). How do I start with the like of this?

POLICEMAN. First you saws . . .

(*She attempts to saw. The beard comes off in her hand.*)

CINDERELLA (*recognising his face*). You!

POLICEMAN (*stepping triumphantly out of his disguise*). Me!

(*As sometimes happens, however, the one who means to give the surprise gets a greater. At sight of his dreaded uniform the child screams, whereat two other children in other boxes bob up and scream also. It is some time before the policeman can speak.*)

So that 's what the boxes was for!

CINDERELLA (*feebly*). Yes.

POLICEMAN (*portentously*). Who and what are these phenomenons?

CINDERELLA (*protectingly*). Don't be frightened, children. Down!

(*They disappear obediently.*)

There 's no wrong in it. They 're just me trying to do my bit. It 's said all should do their bit in war-time. It was into a hospital I wanted to go to nurse the wounded soldiers. I offered myself at every hospital door, but none would have me, so this was all I could do.

POLICEMAN. You 're taking care of them?

(*She nods.*)

Sounds all right. Neighbours' children?

CINDERELLA. The brown box is. She 's half of an orphan, her father's a blue-jacket, so, of course, I said I would.

POLICEMAN. You need say no more. I pass little bluejacket.

CINDERELLA. Those other two is allies. She 's French—and her 's a Belgy. (*Calls.*) Marie-Therese!

(*The French child sits up.*)

Speak your language to the gentleman, Marie-Therese.

MARIE. Bon soir, monsieur—comment portez-vous? Je t'aime. (*She curtsies charmingly to him from the box.*)

POLICEMAN. Well, I 'm —d!

CINDERELLA. Delphine.

(*The Belgian looks up.*)

Make votre bow.

Gladys.

(*The English child bobs up.*)

A friend, Gladys.

(GLADYS *and the* POLICEMAN *grin to each other.*)

GLADYS. What cheer!

CINDERELLA. Monsieur is a Britain's defender.

MARIE. Oh, la, la! Parlez-vous français, monsieur? Non! I blow you two kisses, Monsieur—the one is to you (*kisses hand*) to keep, the other you will give—(*kisses hand*) to Kitch.

POLICEMAN (*writing*). Sends kiss to Lord Kitchener.

CINDERELLA. She 's the one that does most of the talking.

POLICEMAN (*who is getting friendly*). I suppose that other box is an empty.

(CINDERELLA'S *mouth closes.*)

Is that box empty?

CINDERELLA. It 's not exactly empty.

POLICEMAN. What 's inside?

CINDERELLA. She 's the littlest.

(*The children exchange glances and she is severe.*)

Couchy.

(*They disappear.*)

POLICEMAN. An ally?

CINDERELLA. She 's—she 's—Swiss.

POLICEMAN (*lowering*). Now then!

CINDERELLA. She 's not exactly Swiss. You can guess now what she is.

POLICEMAN (*grave*). This puts me in a very difficult position.

CINDERELLA (*beginning to cry*). Nobody would take her. She was left over. I tried not to take her. I 'm a patriot, I am. But there she was—left over—and her so terrible little—I couldn't help taking her.

POLICEMAN. I dunno. (*Quite unfairly.*) If her folk had been in your place and you in hers, they would have shown neither mercy nor pity for you.

CINDERELLA (*stoutly*). That makes no difference.

POLICEMAN (*was this the great moment?*). I think there 's something uncommon about you.

CINDERELLA (*pleased*). About *me* ?

POLICEMAN. I suppose she 's sleeping ?

CINDERELLA. Not her !

POLICEMAN. What 's she doing ?

CINDERELLA. She 's strafing !

POLICEMAN. Who 's she strafing ?

CINDERELLA. Very likely you. She misses nobody. You see I 've put some barb-wire round her box.

POLICEMAN. I see now.

CINDERELLA. It 's not really barb-wire. It 's worsted. I was feared the wire would hurt her. But it just makes a difference.

POLICEMAN. How do the others get on with her ?

CINDERELLA. I makes them get on with her. Of course there 's tongues out, and little things like that.

POLICEMAN. Were the foreign children shy of you at first ?

CINDERELLA. Not as soon as they heard my name. 'Oh, are you Cinderella ?' they said, in their various languages—and 'when 's the ball ?' they said.

POLICEMAN. Somebody must have telled them about you.

CINDERELLA (*happy*). Not here. They had heard about me in their foreign lands. Everybody knows Cinderella: it 's fine. Even her—(*indicating German*) the moment I mentioned my name—' Where 's your ugly sisters ? ' says she, looking round.

POLICEMAN. Sisters ? It 's new to me, your having sisters. (*He produces his note-book.*)

CINDERELLA (*uneasily*). It 's kind of staggering to me, too. I haven't been able to manage them yet, but they 'll be at the ball.

POLICEMAN. It 's queer.

CINDERELLA. It *is* queer.

POLICEMAN (*sitting down with her*). How do you know this ball 's to-night ?

CINDERELLA. It had to be some night. You see, after I closes my business I have chats with the children about things, and naturally it 's mostly about the ball. I put it off as long as I could, but it had to be some night—and this is the night.

POLICEMAN. You mean it 's make-believe ?

CINDERELLA (*almost fiercely*). None of that!

POLICEMAN (*shaking his head*). I don't like it.

CINDERELLA (*shining*). You wouldn't say that if you heard the blasts on the trumpet and loud roars of 'Make way for the Lady Cinderella!'

(*Three heads pop up again.*)

POLICEMAN. Lady?

CINDERELLA (*in a tremble of exultation*). That's me. That's what you're called at royal balls. Then loud huzzas is heard outside from the excited popu-lace, for by this time the fame of my beauty has spread like wild-fire through the streets, and folks is hanging out at windows and climbing lamp-posts to catch a sight of me.

(*Delight of the children.*)

POLICEMAN. My sakes, you see the whole thing clear!

CINDERELLA. I see it from beginning to end—like as if I could touch it—the gold walls and the throne, and the lamp-posts and the horses.

POLICEMAN. The horses?

CINDERELLA. . . . Well, the competitors. The speeches—everything. If only I had my invite! That wasn't a knock at the door, was it?

POLICEMAN (*so carried away that he goes to see*). No.

CINDERELLA (*vindictively*). I dare say that flunkey's sitting drinking in some public-house.

(*Here* MARIE-THERESE *and* GLADYS, *who have been communicating across their boxes, politely invite the* POLICEMAN *to go away.*)

MARIE. Bonne nuit, Monsieur.

GLADYS. Did you say you was going, Mister?

POLICEMAN. They 're wonderful polite.

CINDERELLA. I doubt that 's not politeness. The naughties—they 're asking you to go away.

POLICEMAN. Oh! (*He rises with hauteur.*)

CINDERELLA. You see we 're to have a bite of supper before I start—to celebrate the night.

POLICEMAN. Supper with the kids! When I was a kid in the country at Badgery— You 've done it again!

CINDERELLA. Done what?

POLICEMAN (*with that strange feeling of being at home*). I suppose I would be in the way?

CINDERELLA. There 's not very much to eat. There 's just one for each.

POLICEMAN. I 've had my supper.

CINDERELLA (*seeing her way*). Have you? Then I would be very pleased if you would stay.

POLICEMAN. Thank you kindly.

(*She prepares the table for the feast. Eyes sparkle from the boxes.*)

CINDERELLA (*shining*). This is the first party we 've ever had. Please keep an eye on the door in case there 's a knock.

(*She darts into her bedroom, and her charges are more at their ease.*)

MARIE. (*sitting up, the better to display her nightgown*). Monsieur, Monsieur, voilà!

GLADYS. Cinderella made it out of watching a shop window.

POLICEMAN (*like one who has known his hostess from infancy*). Just like her.

MARIE (*holding up a finger that is adorned with a ring*). Monsieur!

GLADYS (*more practical*). The fire 's going out.

POLICEMAN (*recklessly*). In with another penny. (*He feeds the fire with that noble coin.*)

Fellow allies, I 'm going to take a peep into the German trench! Hah!

(*He stealthily mounts a chair and puts his hand into* GRETCHEN'S *box. We must presume that it is bitten by the invisible occupant, for he withdraws it hurriedly to the hearty delight of the spectators. This mirth changes to rapture as* CINDERELLA *makes a conceited entrance carrying a jug of milk and five hot potatoes in their jackets. Handsomely laden as she is, it is her attire that calls forth the applause. She is now wearing the traditional short brown dress of* CINDERELLA, *and her hair hangs loose. She tries to look modest.*)

CINDERELLA (*displaying herself*). What do you think?

POLICEMAN (*again in Badgery*). Great! Turn round. And I suppose you made it yourself out of a shop window?

CINDERELLA. No, we didn't need no shop window; we all knew exactly what I was wearing when the knock came.

GLADYS. Of course we did.

(*A potato is passed up to each and a cup of milk between two. There is also a delicious saucerful of melted lard into which they dip.* GRETCHEN *is now as much in evidence as the others, and quite as attractive; the fun becomes fast and furious.*)

CINDERELLA (*to* POLICEMAN). A potato?

POLICEMAN. No, I thank you.

CINDERELLA. Just a snack?

POLICEMAN. Thank you.

(*She shares with him.*)

CINDERELLA. A little dip?

POLICEMAN. No, I thank you.

CINDERELLA. Just to look friendly.

POLICEMAN. I thank you. (*Dipping.*) To you, Cinderella.

CINDERELLA. I thank you.

POLICEMAN (*proposing a toast*). The King!

CINDERELLA (*rather consciously*). And the Prince of Wales.

GLADYS. And father.

POLICEMAN. The King, the Prince of Wales, and father.

(*The toast is drunk, dipped and eaten with

acclamation. GLADYS, *uninvited, recites 'The Mariners of England.'* MARIE-THERESE *follows (without waiting for the end) with the Marseillaise, and* GRETCHEN *puts out her tongue at both. Our* POLICEMAN *having intimated that he desires to propose another toast of a more lengthy character, the children are lifted down and placed in their nightgowns at the table.)*

POLICEMAN (*suddenly becoming nervous*). I have now the honour to propose absent friends.

GLADYS (*with an inspiration to which* MARIE-THERESE *bows elegantly*). Vive la France !

POLICEMAN. I mean our friends at the Front. And they have their children, too. Your boxes we know about, but I dare say there 's many similar and even queerer places, where the children, the smallest of our allies, are sleeping this night within the sound of shells.

MARIE. La petite Belgique. La pauvre enfant !

DELPHINE (*proudly*). Me !

POLICEMAN. So here 's to absent friends—

GLADYS (*with another inspiration*). Absent boxes!

POLICEMAN. Absent boxes! And there 's a party we know about who would like uncommon to have the charge of the lot of them—(*looking at* CINDERELLA). And I couples the toast with the name of the said party.

CINDERELLA (*giving a pennyworth for nothing*). Kind friends, it would be pretending of me not to let on that I know I am the party referred to by the last speaker—in far too flattersome words. When I look about me and see just four boxes I am a kind of shamed, but it wasn't very convenient to me to have more. I will now conclude by saying I wish I was the old woman that lived in a shoe, and it doesn't matter how many I had I would have known fine what to do. The end.

(*After further diversion.*) It 's a fine party. I hope your potato is mealy?

POLICEMAN. I never had a better tatie.

CINDERELLA. Don't spare the skins.

POLICEMAN. But you 're eating nothing yourself.

CINDERELLA. I'm not hungry. And, of course, I'll be expected to take a bite at the ball.

(*This reminder of the ball spoils the* POLICEMAN'S *enjoyment.*)

POLICEMAN. I wish—you wasn't so sure of the ball.

GLADYS (*in defence*). Why shouldn't she not be sure of it ?

DELPHINE. Pourquoi, Monsieur ?

CINDERELLA (*rather hotly*). Don't say things like that here.

MARIE. Has Monsieur by chance seen God-mamma coming ?

POLICEMAN. God-mamma ?

CINDERELLA. That 's my Godmother ; she brings my ball dress and a carriage with four ponies.

GLADYS. Then away she goes to the ball—hooray—hooray !

CINDERELLA. It 's all perfectly simple once Godmother comes.

POLICEMAN (*with unconscious sarcasm*). I can see she 's important.

CINDERELLA (*with the dreadful sinking that*

comes to her at times.) You think she 'll come, don't you ?

POLICEMAN. Cinderella, your hand 's burning —and in this cold room.

CINDERELLA. Say you think she 'll come.

POLICEMAN. I—well, I . . . I . . .

GLADYS (*imploringly*). Say it, Mister !

DELPHINE (*begging*). Monsieur ! Monsieur !

MARIE. If it is that you love me, Monsieur !

POLICEMAN (*in distress*). I question if there was ever before a member of the Force in such a position. (*Yielding.*) I expect she 'll come.

(*This settles it in the opinion of the children, but their eyes are too bright for such a late hour, and they are ordered to bed. Our* POLICEMAN *replaces them in their boxes.*)

CINDERELLA. One—two—three . . . couchy !

(*They disappear.*)

POLICEMAN (*awkwardly and trying to hedge*). Of course this is an out-of-the-way little street for a Godmother to find.

CINDERELLA. Yes, I 've thought of that. I 'd best go and hang about outside ; she would know me by my dress.

POLICEMAN (*hastily*). I wouldn't do that. It 's a cold night. (*He wanders about the room eyeing her sideways.*) Balls is always late things.

CINDERELLA. I 'm none so sure. In war-time, you see, with the streets so dark and the King so kind, it would be just like him to begin early and close at ten instead of twelve. I must leave before twelve. If I don't, there 's terrible disasters happens.

POLICEMAN (*unable to follow this*). The ball might be put off owing to the Prince of Wales being in France.

CINDERELLA. He catched the last boat. I 'll go out and watch.

POLICEMAN (*desperate*). Stay where you are, and—and I 'll have a look for her.

CINDERELLA. You 're too kind.

POLICEMAN. Not at all. I must be stepping at any rate. If I can lay hands on her I 'll march her here, though I have to put the hand-cuffs on her.

GLADYS (*looking up*). I think I heard a knock!

(*The* POLICEMAN *looks out, shakes his head, and finally departs after a queer sort of handshake with* MISS THING.)

CINDERELLA. He 's a nice man.

GLADYS. Have you known him long ?

CINDERELLA (*thinking it out*). A longish time. He 's head of the secret police ; him and me used to play together as children down in Badgery. His folks live in a magnificent castle, with two doors. (*She becomes a little bewildered.*) I 'm all mixed up.

(*The children are soon asleep. She wanders aimlessly to the door. The wall closes on the little room, and we now see her standing in the street. Our* POLICEMAN *returns and flashes his lantern on her.*)

CINDERELLA. It 's you !

POLICEMAN. It 's me. But there 's no Godmother. There 's not a soul . . . No. . . . Good-night, Cinderella. Go inside.

CINDERELLA (*doggedly*). Not me ! I don't feel the cold—not much. And one has to take risks to get a Prince. The only thing I 'm feared about is my feet. If they was to swell I mightn't be able to get the slippers on, and he would have naught to do with me.

POLICEMAN. What slippers? If you won't go back, I'll stop here with you.

CINDERELLA. No, I think there's more chance of her coming if I'm alone.

POLICEMAN. I'm very troubled about you.

CINDERELLA (*wistfully*). Do you think I'm just a liar? Maybe I am. You see I'm all mixed up. I'm sore in need of somebody to help me out.

POLICEMAN. I would do it if I could.

CINDERELLA. I'm sure. (*Anxiously.*) Are you good at riddles?

(*He shakes his head.*)

There's always a riddle before you can marry into a royal family.

POLICEMAN (*with increased gloom*). The whole thing seems to be most terrible difficult.

CINDERELLA. Yes. . . . Good-night.

POLICEMAN. You won't let me stay with you?

CINDERELLA. No.

(*He puts his lantern on the ground beside her.*)

What 's that for ?

POLICEMAN (*humbly*). It 's just a sort of guard for you. (*He takes off his muffler and puts it several times round her neck.*)

CINDERELLA. Nice !

POLICEMAN. Good luck.

(*She finds it easiest just to nod in reply.*)

I wish I was a Prince.

CINDERELLA (*suddenly struck by the idea*). You 're kind of like him.

(*He goes away. She sits down on the step to wait. She shivers. She takes the muffler off her neck and winds it round her more valuable feet. She falls asleep.*

Darkness comes, and snow. From somewhere behind, the shadowy figure of CINDERELLA'S *Godmother, beautiful in a Red Cross Nurse's uniform, is seen looking benignantly on the waif.* CINDERELLA *is just a little vague, huddled form—there is no movement.*)

GODMOTHER. Cinderella, my little godchild !

CINDERELLA (*with eyes unopening*). Is that you, Godmother ?

GODMOTHER. It is I; my poor god-daughter is all mixed up, and I have come to help her out.

CINDERELLA. You have been long in coming. I very near gave you up.

GODMOTHER. Sweetheart, I couldn't come sooner, because in these days, you know, even the fairy godmother is with the Red Cross.

CINDERELLA. Was that the reason? I see now; I thought perhaps you kept away because I wasn't a good girl.

GODMOTHER. You have been a good brave girl; I am well pleased with my darling godchild.

CINDERELLA. It is fine to be called darling; it heats me up. I 've been wearying for it, Godmother. Life 's a kind of hard.

GODMOTHER. It will always be hard to you, Cinderella. I can't promise you anything else.

CINDERELLA. I don't suppose I could have my three wishes, Godmother.

GODMOTHER. I am not very powerful in these days, Cinderella; but what are your wishes?

CINDERELLA. I would like fine to have my ball, Godmother.

GODMOTHER. You shall have your ball.

CINDERELLA. I would like to nurse the wounded.

GODMOTHER. You shall nurse the wounded.

CINDERELLA. I would like to be loved by the man of my choice, Godmother.

GODMOTHER. You shall be loved by the man of your choice.

CINDERELLA. Thank you kindly. The ball first, if you please, and could you squeeze in the children so that they may see me in my glory.

GODMOTHER. Now let this be my down-trodden godchild's ball, not as balls are, but as they are conceived to be in a little chamber in Cinderella's head.

(*She fades from sight. In the awful stillness we can now hear the tiny clatter of horses infinitely small and infinitely far off. It is the equipage of* CINDERELLA. *Then an unearthly trumpet sounds thrice, and the darkness is blown away.*

It is the night of the most celebrated ball in history, and we see it through our heroine's eyes. She has, as it were, made everything with her own hands, from the cloths of gold to the ices.

Nearly everything in the ball-room is of gold: it was only with an effort that she checked herself from dabbing gold on the regal countenances. You can see that she has not passed by gin-palaces without thinking about them. The walls and furniture are so golden that you have but to lean against them to acquire a competency. There is a golden throne with gold cloths on it, and the royal seats are three golden rocking chairs; there would be a fourth golden rocking chair if it were not that CINDERELLA *does not want you to guess where she is to sit. These chairs are stuffed to a golden corpulency. The panoply of the throne is about twenty feet high—each foot of pure gold; and nested on the top of it is a golden reproduction of the grandest thing* CINDERELLA *has ever seen—the private box of a theatre. In this box sit, wriggle, and sprawl the four children in their night-gowns, leaning over the golden parapet as if to the manner born and carelessly kicking nuggets out of it. They are shouting, pointing, and otherwise behaving badly, eating oranges out of paper bags, then blowing out the bags and bursting them. The superb scene is lit by four street lamps with red glass. Dancing is going on: the ladies all in white, the gentlemen in black with swords. If you were unused to royal balls you would think every one of these people was worth describing separately; but, compared to what is coming, it may be said that* CINDERELLA *has merely pushed them on with her lovely foot. They are her idea of courtiers, and have anxious expressions as if they knew she was watching them. They have character in the lump, if we may put it that way, but none individually. Thus one cannot smile or sigh, for instance, without all the others smiling or sighing. At night they probably sleep in two large beds, one for ladies and one for gentlemen, and if one of the ladies, say, wants to turn round, she gives the signal, and they all turn simul-*

taneously. As children they were not like this ; they had genuine personal traits, but these have gradually been blotted out as they basked in royal favour ; thus, if the KING *wipes his glasses they all pretend that their glasses need wiping, and when the* QUEEN *lets her handkerchief fall they all stoop loyally to pick up their own.*

Down the golden steps at the back comes the LORD MAYOR, *easily recognisable by his enormous chain.*)

LORD MAYOR. O yes, O yes, make way every one for the Lord Mayor—namely myself.

(*They all make way for him. Two black boys fling open lovely curtains.*)

O yes, O yes, make way every one, and also myself, for Lord Times.

(*This is a magnificent person created by* CINDERELLA *on learning from* MR. BODIE *that the press is all powerful and that the 'Times' is the press. He carries one hand behind his back, as if it might be too risky to show the whole of himself at once, and it is noticeable that as he walks his feet do not quite touch the ground. He is the only person who is not a little staggered by the amount of gold: you almost feel that he thinks there is not quite enough of it. He very nearly sits down on one of the royal rocking chairs: and the* LORD MAYOR, *looking red and unhappy, and as if he had now done for himself, has to whisper to him that the seats under the throne are reserved.*)

O yes, O yes, make way for the Censor.

(CINDERELLA *has had a good deal of trouble over this person, of whom she has heard a great deal in war-time, without meeting any one who can tell her what he is like. She has done her best, and he is long and black and thin, dressed as tightly as a fish, and carries an executioner's axe. All fall back from him in fear, except* LORD TIMES, *who takes a step forward, and then the* CENSOR *falls back.*)

O yes, O yes, make way everybody for his Royal Highness the King, and his good lady the Queen.

(*The* KING *and* QUEEN *are attired like their*

portraits on playing cards, who are the only royalties CINDERELLA *has seen, and they advance grandly to their rocking chairs, looking as if they thought the whole public was dirt, but not so much despised dirt as dirt with good points.* LORD TIMES *fixes them with his eye, and the* KING *hastily crosses and shakes hands with him.*)

O yes, O yes, Make way every one, except the King, and Queen, and Lord Times, for His Highness Prince Hard-to-Please.

(*The heir apparent comes, preceded by trumpeters. His dress may a little resemble that of the extraordinary youth seen by* CINDERELLA *in her only pantomime, but what quite takes our breath away is his likeness to our* POLICEMAN. *If the ball had taken place a night earlier it may be hazarded that the* PRINCE *would have presented quite a different face. It is as if* CINDERELLA'S *views of his personality had undergone some unaccountable change, confusing even to herself, and for a moment the whole scene rocks, the street lamps wink, and odd shadows stalk among the courtiers, shadows of* MR. BODIE, MARION, *and the party in an unfinished coat, who have surely no right to be here. This is only momentarily; then the palace steadies itself again.*

The KING *rises, and in stately manner addresses his guests in the words* CINDERELLA *conceives to be proper to his royal mouth. As he stands waiting superbly for the applause to cease, he holds on to a strap hanging conveniently above his head. To* CINDERELLA *strap-hanging on the Underground has been a rare and romantic privilege.)*

KING. My loyal subjects, all 'ail! I am as proud of you as you are of me. It gives me and my good lady much pleasure to see you 'ere by special invite, feasting at our expense. There is a paper bag for each, containing two sandwiches, buttered on both sides, a piece of cake, a hard-boiled egg, and an orange or a banana.

(The cheers of the delighted courtiers gratify him, but the vulgar children over his head continue their rub-a-dub on the parapet

until he glares up at them. Even then they continue.)

Ladies and Gents all, pleasant though it is to fill up with good victuals, that is not the chief object of this royal invite. We are 'ere for a solemn purpose, namely, to find a mate for our noble son. All the Beauties are waiting in the lobby: no wonder he is excited.

(*All look at the* PRINCE, *who is rocking and yawning.*)

He will presently wake up; but first I want to say—(*here he becomes conscious of* LORD TIMES). What is it?

LORD TIMES. Less talk.

KING. Certainly. (*He sits down.*)

PRINCE (*encouraged to his feet by various royal nudges*). My liege King and Queen-Mother, you can have the competitors brought in, and I will take a look at them; but I have no hope. My curse is this, that I am a scoffer about females. I can play with them for an idle hour and then cast them from me even as I cast this banana skin. I can find none so lovely that I may love her for aye from the depths of my passionate heart. I am so blasted particular. O yes! O yes! (*He sits down and looks helpless.*)

KING (*undismayed*). All ready?

(*The* LORD MAYOR *bows.*)

All is ready, my son.

PRINCE (*bored*). Then let loose the Beauts.

(*To heavenly music from the royal hurdy-gurdies the Beauties descend the stairs, one at a time. There are a dozen of the fine creatures, in impudent confections such as* CINDERELLA *has seen in papers in* MR. BODIE'S *studio; some of them with ropes of hair hanging down their proud backs as she has seen them in a hair-dresser's window. As we know, she has once looked on at a horse show, and this has coloured her conception of a competition for a prince. The ladies prance round the ball-room like high-stepping steeds; it is evident that* CINDERELLA *has had them fed immediately before releasing them; her pride is to show them at their very best, and then to challenge them.*

They paw the floor wantonly until LORD

TIMES *steps forward. Peace thus restored,* HIS MAJESTY *proceeds.)*

KING. The first duty of a royal consort being to be *good,* the test of goodness will now be applied by the Lord Mayor. Every competitor who does not pass in goodness will be made short work of.

(Several ladies quake, and somewhere or other unseen CINDERELLA *is chuckling.)*

ONE OF THE STEEDS. I wasn't told about this. It isn't fair.

LORD MAYOR *(darkly).* If your Grace wishes to withdraw—

(She stamps.)

KING. The Lord Mayor will now apply the test.

LORD MAYOR *(to a gold* PAGE*).* The therm-mo-ometers, boy.

(A whole boxful of thermometers is presented to him by the PAGE *on bended knee. The* LORD MAYOR *is now in his element. He has ridden in gold coaches and knows what hussies young women often are. To dainty music he trips up the line of Beauties*

and pops a tube into each pouting mouth. The competitors circle around, showing their paces while he stands, watch in hand, giving them two minutes. Then airily he withdraws the tubes ; he is openly gleeful when he finds sinners. Twice he is in doubt, it is a very near thing, and he has to consult the KING *in whispers : the* KING *takes the* QUEEN *aside, to whisper behind the door as it were ; then they both look at* LORD TIMES, *who, without even stepping forward, says 'No'—and the doubtfuls are at once bundled out of the chamber with the certainties. Royalty sighs, and the courtiers sigh and the* LORD MAYOR *sighs in a perfunctory way, but there is a tossing of manes from the Beauties who have scraped through.*)

KING (*stirring up the* PRINCE, *who has fallen asleep*). Our Royal Bud will now graciously deign to pick out a few possibles.

(*His Royal Highness yawns.*)

LORD MAYOR (*obsequiously*). If your Highness would like a little assistance—

PRINCE (*you never know how they will take

things). We shall do this for ourselves, my good fellow.

(*He smacks the* LORD MAYOR'S *face with princely elegance. The* LORD MAYOR *takes this as a favour, and the courtiers gently smack each other's faces, and are very proud to be there. The* PRINCE *moves languidly down the line of Beauties considering their charms, occasionally nodding approval but more often screwing up his nose. The courtiers stand ready with nods or noses. Several ladies think they have been chosen, but he has only brought them into prominence to humiliate them ; he suddenly says 'Good-bye,' and they have to go, while he is convulsed with merriment. He looks sharply at the courtiers to see if they are convulsed also, and most of them are. The others are flung out.*)

QUEEN (*hanging on to her strap*). Does our Royal one experience no palpitation at all ?

PRINCE (*sleepily*). Ah me, ah me!

LORD TIMES (*irritated*). You are well called 'Ard-to-Please. You would turn up your nose at a lady though she were shaped like Apollo's bow.

(*The* PRINCE *shrugs his shoulder to indicate that love cannot be forced.*)

LORD MAYOR (*darkly*). And now we come to the severer test.

(*With a neat action, rather like taking a lid off a pot, the* LORD MAYOR *lets it be known to the ladies that they must now lift their skirts to show their feet. When this devastating test is concluded, there are only two competitors left in the room.*)

LORD TIMES (*almost as if he were thinking of himself*). Can't have Two.

(*Cards such as* CINDERELLA *saw at the horse show, with* '1st,' '2nd,' *and* '3rd' *on them, are handed to the* PRINCE. *Like one well used to such proceedings, he pins* 2nd *and* 3rd *into the ladies' bodices.*)

QUEEN (*gloomily*). But still no first.

(*The children applaud; they have been interfering repeatedly.*)

KING. Come, come, proud youth, you feel no palps at all?

PRINCE. Not a palp. Perhaps for a moment this one's nose—that one's cock of the head—But it has passed.

(*He drearily resumes his rocking chair. No one seems to know what to do next.*)

MARIE (*to the rescue*). The two Ugly Sisters! Monsieur le Roi, the two Ugly Sisters! (*She points derisively at the winners.*)

KING (*badgered*). How did these children get their invites?

(*This is another thing that no one knows. Once more the room rocks, and* MR. BODIE *passes across it as if looking for some one. Then a growing clamour is heard outside. Bugles sound. The* LORD MAYOR *goes, and returns with strange news.*)

LORD MAYOR. Another competitor, my King. Make way for the Lady Cinderella.

KING. Cinderella? I don't know her.

GLADYS (*nearly falling out of the box*). You 'll soon know her. Now you 'll see! Somebody wake the Prince up!

(*The portals are flung open, and* CINDERELLA *is seen alighting from her lovely equipage, which we will not describe because some one has described it before. But note the little waggle of her foot just before she favours the ground. We have thought a great deal about how our* CINDERELLA *should be dressed for this occasion: white of course, and she looked a darling in it, but we boggle at its really being of the grandest stuff and made in the shop where the Beauties got theirs. No, the material came from poorer warehouses in some shabby district not far from the street of the penny shop; her eyes had glistened as she gazed at it through the windows, and she paid for it with her life's blood, and made the frock herself. Very possibly it was bunchy here and there.*

CINDERELLA *then comes sailing down into the ball-room, not a sound to be heard except the ecstatic shrieks of the four children. She is modest but calmly confident; she knows exactly what to do. She moves once round the room to show her gown, then curtsies to the Royal personages; then, turning to the* LORD MAYOR, *opens her mouth and signs to him to pop in the thermometer. He does it as in a dream. Presently he is excitedly showing the thermometer to the* KING.)

KING. Marvellous! 99!

(*The cry is repeated from all sides. The* QUEEN *hands the* KING *a long pin from her coiffure, and the* PRINCE *is again wakened.*)

PRINCE (*with his hand to his brow*). What, another! Oh, all right; but you know this is a dog's life. (*He goes to* CINDERELLA, *takes one glance at her and resumes his chair.*)

LORD MAYOR (*while the children blub*). That settles it, I think. (*He is a heartless fellow.*) That will do. Stand back, my girl.

CINDERELLA (*calmly*). I don't think.

KING. It 's no good, you know.

CINDERELLA (*curtsying*). Noble King, there is two bits of me thy son hath not yet seen. I crave my rights. (*She points to the two bits referred to, which are encased in the loveliest glass slippers.*)

KING. True. Boy, do your duty.

PRINCE. Oh, bother!

(*Those words are the last spoken by him in his present state. When we see him again, which is the moment afterwards, he is translated. He looks the same, but so does a clock into which new works have been put. The change is effected quite simply by* CINDERELLA *delicately raising her skirt and showing him her foot. As the exquisite nature of the sight thus vouchsafed to him penetrates his being a tremor passes through his frame; his vices take flight from him and the virtues enter. It is a heady wakening, and he falls at her feet. The courtiers are awkward, not knowing whether they should fall also.* CINDERELLA *beams to the children, who utter ribald cries of triumph.*)

KING (*rotating on his strap*). Give him air. Fill your lungs, my son.

QUEEN (*on hers*). My boy! My boy!

LORD MAYOR (*quickly taking the royal cue*). Oh, lady fair!

(*The* PRINCE'S *palpitations increase in violence.*)

QUEEN. Oh, happy sight!

KING. Oh, glorious hour!

LORD MAYOR (*not sure that he was heard the first time*). Oh, lady fair!

(*The* PRINCE *springs to his feet. He is looking very queer.*)

LORD TIMES (*probably remembering how he looked once*). The Prince is about to propose.

LORD MAYOR. O yes, O yes, O yes!

KING. Proceed, my son.

PRINCE (*with lover-like contortions and addressing himself largely to the feet*). Dew of the morning, garden of delight, sweet petals of enchanted nights, the heavens have opened and through the chink thou hast fallen at my feet, even as I fall at thine. Thou art not one but twain, and these the twain—Oh, pretty feet on which my lady walks, are they but feet? O no, O no, O no! They are so small I cannot see them. Hie! A candle that I may see my lady's feet!

(*He kisses one foot, and she holds up the other for similar treatment.*)

O Cinderella, if thou wilt deign to wife with me, I 'll do my best to see that through the years you always walk on kisses.

(*The courtiers resolve to walk on kisses for evermore.*)

LORD MAYOR. The Prince has proposed. The Lady Cinderella will now reply.

KING. Lovely creature, take pity on my royal son.

QUEEN. Cinderella, be my daughter.

LORD TIMES (*succinctly*). Yes, or no ?

CINDERELLA. There 's just one thing. Before I answer, I would like that little glass thing to be put in his mouth.

LORD MAYOR (*staggered*). The Ther-mo-mometer ?

KING. In our *Prince's* mouth !

LORD TIMES. Why not ?

CINDERELLA. Just to make sure that he is good.

PRINCE (*with a sinking*). Oh, I say !

QUEEN. Of course he is good, Cinderella—he is our son.

CINDERELLA (*doggedly*). I would like it put in his mouth.

KING. But—

PRINCE (*alarmed*). Pater!

LORD TIMES. It must be done.

(*The test is therefore made. The royal mouth has to open to the thermometer, which is presently passed to the* KING *for examination. He looks very grave. The* PRINCE *seizes the tell-tale thing, and with a happy thought lets it fall.*)

PRINCE. 99!

(*The joyous cry is taken up by all, and* CINDERELLA *goes divinely on one knee to her lord and master.*)

CINDERELLA (*simply*). I accepts.

KING (*when the uproar has ceased*). All make merry. The fire is going low. (*Recklessly.*) In with another shilling!

(*A shilling is dumped into the shilling-in-the-slot stove, which blazes up. The* PRINCE *puts his arm round his love.*)

LORD TIMES (*again remembering his day of days*). My Prince, not so fast. There is still the riddle.

PRINCE. I had forgotten.

CINDERELLA (*quaking*). I was feared there would be a riddle.

KING (*prompted by* LORD TIMES). Know ye all, my subjects, that before blue blood can wed there is a riddle; and she who cannot guess it—(*darkly*) is taken away and censored.

(*The* CENSOR *with his axe comes into sudden prominence behind* CINDERELLA *and the two other competitors.*)

My Lord Times, the riddle.

LORD TIMES. I hold in my one hand the riddle, and in the other the answer in a sealed envelope, to prevent any suspicion of hanky-panky. Third prize, forward. Now, my child, this is the riddle. On the night of the Zeppelin raids, what was it that every one rushed to save first?

3RD PRIZE. The children.

LORD TIMES. Children not included.

(*The lady is at a loss.*)

PRINCE. Time 's up! Hoo-ray!

(*He signs callously to the* CENSOR, *who disappears with his victim through a side door, to reappear presently, alone, wiping his axe and skipping gaily.*)

LORD TIMES. Second prize, forward. Now, Duchess, answer.

2ND PRIZE. Her jewels.

(LORD TIMES *shakes his head.*)

PRINCE (*brightly*). Off with her head. Drown her in a bucket.

(*The* CENSOR *again removes the lady and does his fell work.*)

LORD TIMES. First prize, forward. Now, Cinderella, answer.

(*The* CENSOR, *a kindly man but used to his calling, puts his hand on her shoulder, to lead her away. She removes it without looking at him.*)

CINDERELLA. It 's not a catch, is it ?

LORD TIMES (*hotly*). No, indeed.

CINDERELLA. There 's just one thing all true Britons would be anxious about.

KING (*who has been allowed to break the envelope and read the answer*). But what, Cinderella—what ?

LORD MAYOR (*hedging again*). What, chit ?

CINDERELLA. Their love-letters.

KING and LORD TIMES (*together, but* LORD TIMES

a little in front). The fair Cinderella has solved the riddle!

LORD MAYOR (*promptly*). Oh, fair lady!

CINDERELLA (*remembering the Venus*). There's just one thing that makes it not quite a perfect ball. I wanted Mrs. Bodie to be one of the competitors—so as I could beat her.

KING. Send for her at once. Take a taxi.

(*A courtier rushes out whistling, and returns with* VENUS, *now imbued with life. Her arms go out wantonly to the* PRINCE. *He signs to the* CENSOR, *who takes her away and breaks her up.*)

PRINCE. I crave a boon. The wedding at once, my lord.

(LORD TIMES *signifies assent.*)

KING. The marriage ceremony will now take place.

CINDERELLA (*calling to the children*). Bridesmaids!

(*They rush down and become her bridesmaids. At the top of the stair appears a penguin—a penguin or a bishop, they melt into each other on great occasions. The regal couple kneel.)*

PENGUIN. Do you, O Prince, take this lady to be your delightful wife—and to adore her for ever?

PRINCE. I do, I do! Oh, I do, I do indeed! I do—I do—I do!

PENGUIN. Do you, Cinderella, loveliest of your sex, take this Prince for husband, and to love, honour, and obey him?

CINDERELLA (*primly*). If you please.

PENGUIN. The ring?

(*It is* MARIE-THERESE'S *great hour; she passes her ring to* CINDERELLA, *who is married in it. Triumphant music swells out as a crown is put upon our Princess's head, and an extraordinarily long train attached to her person. Her husband and she move dreamily round the ball-room, the children holding up the train.* LORD TIMES *with exquisite taste falls in behind them. Then follow the courtiers, all dreamily; and completing the noble procession is the* LORD MAYOR, *holding aloft on a pole an enormous penny. It has the face of* CINDERELLA *on one side of it— the penny which to those who know life is the most romantic of coins unless its little brother has done better.*

The music, despite better intentions, begins to lose its head. It obviously wants to dance. Every one wants to dance. Even LORD TIMES *has trouble with his legs.*)

KING (*threatening, supplicating*). Don't dance yet. I 've got a surprise for you. Don't dance. I haven't told you about it, so as to keep you on the wonder.

(*In vain do they try to control themselves.*)

It 's ices !

(*All stop dancing.*)

(*Hoarsely*). There 's an ice-cream for everybody.

(*Amid applause the royal ice-cream barrow is wheeled on by haughty menials who fill the paper sieves with dabs of the luscious condiment. The paper sieves are of gold, but there are no spoons. The children, drunk with expectation, forget their manners and sit on the throne. Somehow* CINDERELLA'S *penny clients drift in again, each carrying a sieve.*)

None touches till one royal lick has been taken by us four. . . . (*He gives them a toast.*) To the Bridal Pair!

(*At the royal word 'Go!' all attack the ices with their tongues, greedily but gracefully. They end in the approved manner by gobbling up the sieves. It is especially charming to see the last of* LORD TIMES'S *sieve. The music becomes irresistible. If you did not dance you would be abandoned by your legs. It is as if a golden coin had been dropped into a golden slot. Ranks are levelled. The* KING *asks* GLADYS *for this one; the* QUEEN *is whisked away by* MR. BODIE. *Perhaps they dance like costers: if you had time to reflect you might think it a scene in the streets. It becomes too merry to last; couples are whirled through the walls as if the floor itself were rotating: soon* CINDERELLA *and her* PRINCE *dance alone. It is then that the clock begins to strike twelve.* CINDERELLA *should fly now, or woe befall her. Alas, she hears nothing save the whispers of her lover. The hour has struck, and her glorious gown shrinks slowly into the tattered frock of a girl with a broom. Too late she huddles on the floor to conceal the change. In another moment the* PRINCE *must see. The children gather round her with little cries, and, spreading out their night-gowns to conceal her, rush her from the scene. It is then that the* PRINCE *discovers his loss. In a frenzy he calls her sweet name. The bewildered girl has even forgotten to drop the slipper, without which he shall never find her.* MARIE-THERESE, *the ever-vigilant, steals back with it, and leaves it on the floor.*

The ball-room is growing dark. The lamps have gone out. There is no light save the tiniest glow, which has been showing on the floor all the time, unregarded by us. It seems to come from a policeman's lantern. The gold is all washed out by the odd streaks of white that come down like rain. Soon the PRINCE'S *cry of 'Cinderella, Cinderella' dies away. It is no longer a ball-room on which the lantern sheds this feeble ray. is the street outside* CINDERELLA'S *door, a white street now, silent in snow. The child in her rags, the* POLICEMAN'S *scarf still round her precious feet, is asleep on the doorstep, very little life left in her, very little oil left in the lantern.)*

III

The retreat in which Cinderella is to be found two months later has been described to us by our policeman with becoming awe. It seems to be a very pleasant house near the sea, and possibly in pre-war days people were at ease in it. None of that, says the policeman emphatically, with Dr. Bodie in charge. He could wink discreetly at Dr. Bodie in absence, but was prepared to say on oath that no one ever winked at her when she was present. In the old days he had been more than a passive observer of the suffragette in action, had even been bitten by them in the way of business; had not then gone into the question of their suitability for the vote, but liked the pluck of them; had no objection to his feelings on the woman movement being summed up in this way, that he had vaguely disapproved of their object, but had admired their methods. After knowing Dr. Bodie he must admit that his views about their object had undergone a change; was now a whole-hearted supporter, felt in his bones that Dr. Bodie was born to command: astonishing thing about her that she did it so natural-

like. She was not in the least mannish or bullying; she was a very ladylike sort of person, a bit careful about the doing of her hair, and the set of her hat, and she had a soft voice, though what you might call an arbitrary manner. Very noticeable the way she fixed you with her steely eye. In appearance she was very like her room at the retreat, or the room was very like her; everything in cruel good order, as you might say; an extraordinarily decorous writing-table near the centre, the sort of table against which you instinctively stood and waited to make your deposition; the friendliest thing in the room (to a policeman) was the book-cases with wire doors, because the books looked through the wires at you in a homely way like prisoners. It was a sunny room at times, but this did not take away from its likeness to the doctor, who could also smile on occasion.

Into this room Mr. Bodie is shown on a summer afternoon by a maid with no nonsense about her in working hours.

MAID (*who knows that male visitors should be impressed at once*). This way, sir; I shall see whether Dr. Bodie is disengaged.

BODIE (*doggedly*). *Miss* Bodie.

MAID (*with firm sweetness*). Dr. Bodie, sir. What name shall I say ?

BODIE (*wincing*). Mr. Bodie ; her brother.

MAID (*unmoved*). I shall tell Dr. Bodie, sir.

BODIE (*a fighter to the last*). Miss Bodie.

MAID. Dr. Bodie, sir.

(*He is surveying the room with manly disapproval when his sister appears and greets him. She is all that the* POLICEMAN *has said of her, and more ; if we did not have a heroine already we would chose* DR. BODIE. *At the same time it cannot be denied that she is enough to make any brother wince. For instance, immediately she has passed him the time of day, she seems to be considering his case. Perhaps this is because she has caught him frowning at her stethoscope. There is certainly a twinkle somewhere about her face. Before he can step back indignantly she raises one of his eyelids and comes to a conclusion.*)

DR. BODIE. Oh dear ! Well, Dick, it 's entirely your own fault.

(MR. BODIE *has a curious trick of kicking*

backwards with one foot when people take liberties with him, and a liberty has been taken with him now.)

Kick away, Dick, but you needn't pretend that you have no faith in me as a medical man; for when you are really ill you always take the first train down here. In your heart I am the only doctor you believe in.

BODIE. Stuff, Nellie.

DR. BODIE. Then why did you put Cinderella under my care?

BODIE. I didn't know where else to send her when she was discharged from the hospital. Had to give her a chance of picking up. (*Thawing.*) It was good of you to give her board and lodging.

DR. BODIE (*sitting down to her day-book*). Not at all. I'll send you in a whacking bill for her presently.

BODIE (*kicking*). Well, I've come all this way to see her. How is she getting on, Nellie?

DR. BODIE. She is in the garden. I dare say you can see her from the window.

BODIE. I see some men only; I believe they are wounded Tommies.

DR. BODIE. Yes. There is a Convalescent Home down here. That is part of my job. Do the men look as if they were gathering round anything ?

BODIE. They do.

DR. BODIE. Ah ! Then that is Cinderella. She is now bossing the British Army, Dick.

BODIE. I might have guessed it. (*Chuckling.*) Does she charge a penny ?

DR. BODIE. Not to the military.

BODIE. Nellie, I have had some inquiries made lately about her parents.

DR. BODIE. She doesn't know much about them herself.

BODIE. No, and we needn't tell her this. Her mother—ah well, poor soul !—and the father was a very bad egg. And from that soil, Nellie, this flower has sprung. Nobody to tend it. Can't you see little Cinderella with her watering-can carefully bringing up herself. I wish I could paint that picture.

(*Perhaps* DR. BODIE *sees the picture even more clearly than he does.*)

I see her now. She is on a bed, Nellie.

DR. BODIE. Yes. That is for convenience, for wheeling her about.

BODIE (*waving*). She sees me. And how is she, Nell ?

DR. BODIE. She is always bright; perhaps too bright.

BODIE. Can't be too bright.

DR. BODIE (*controlling her feelings*). A girl who is found frozen in the street by a policeman and taken to a London Hospital, where she has pneumonia—poor little waif! You know, she is very frail, Dick.

BODIE. I know; but she will get better, won't she ?

(*He has said it confidently, but his sister looks at him and turns away. He is startled.*)

Come, Nellie, she is going to get better, isn't she ?

DR. BODIE (*shaking her head*). There isn't much chance, Dick. Her body and soul have had to do too long without the little things they needed.

BODIE. She shall have them now, I promise. What are they ?

DR. BODIE. First of all, just food. She has been half starved all her life. And then human affection. She has been starved of that also; she who has such a genius for it.

(*She goes to the window and calls.*)

No. 7, bring Cinderella in here

(CINDERELLA *in her bed is wheeled in through the window by the soldier,* DANNY. *She is wearing a probationer's cap and dressing jacket. The bed is a simple iron one, small and low, of the kind that was so common in war hospitals; it is on tiny pneumatic wheels with ball bearings for easy propulsion. Though frail,* CINDERELLA *is full of glee.*)

BODIE. Hurray, Cinderella!

CINDERELLA. Hurray! Isn't it lovely. I'm glad you've seen me in my carriage. When I saw there was a visitor I thought at first it might be David.

BODIE. David? I didn't know you . . . Is he a relative?

(CINDERELLA *finds this extremely funny—*

so does DANNY; *even the* DOCTOR *is discreetly amused.*)

CINDERELLA (*to* DANNY). Tell the men that! He 's not exactly a relative. (*She pulls* MR. BODIE *down by the lapels of his coat.*) He 's just that great big ridiculous policeman!

BODIE. Oho! Our policeman again. Does he come all this way to see you?

CINDERELLA (*her shoulders rising in pride*). Twice already; and he 's coming again to-day. Mr. Bodie, get the Doctor to take you over the Convalescent Home. There 's a field with cows in it, a whole litter of them! And the larder? There 's barrel upon barrel full of eggs and sawdust, and Danny says—this is Danny—

(DANNY, *who is slightly lame and is in hospital blue, comes to attention*).

Danny says the hens lay in the barrels so as to save time in packing.

(DANNY *finds the severe eye of the Doctor upon him and is abashed.*)

Mr. Bodie, look! (*displaying her cap*). The Doctor lets me wear it; it makes me half a nurse, a kind of nurse's help. I make bandages, and they 're took away in glass bottles and sterilized. Mr. Bodie, as sure as death I 'm doing something for my country.

DR. BODIE. Cinderella, you 're talking too much.

CINDERELLA (*subsiding meekly*). Yes, Doctor.

DR. BODIE. Dick, I am going over to the hospital presently. If you like to come with me—*really* want to see it—no affected interest—

BODIE. Thanks, I should like it—Dr. Bodie.

DR. BODIE (*to* DANNY). You are not required any more, No. 7.

(DANNY *is going thankfully, but she suddenly pulls him forward to examine his face*).

No. 7, you are wearing that brown eye again.

DANNY (*who has a glass eye*). Yes, Doctor; you see it 's like this. First they sent me a brown eye. Then some meddlesome person finds out my natural eye is blue. So then they sends me a blue eye.

DOCTOR. Yes, where is it?

DANNY. It was a beautiful eye, Doctor; but I had taken a fancy to little browny. And I have a young lady; so I took the liberty of having the blue eye made up into a brooch and I sent it to her.

DR. BODIE (*without moving a muscle*). I shall report you.

BODIE (*when the martinet and* DANNY *have gone*). Are you afraid of her, Cinderella? I am.

CINDERELLA. No! She sometimes dashes me, but she is a fearful kind lady. (*She pulls him down again for further important revelations.*) She 's very particular about her feet.

BODIE (*staggered*). Is she! In a feminine way?

CINDERELLA. Yes.

BODIE. Hurray! Then I have her. The Achilles Heel! (*He is once more jerked down.*)

CINDERELLA. I have a spring bed.

BODIE. Ah!

CINDERELLA (*in some awe*). The first time I woke in hospital, an angel with streamers was standing there holding a tray in her hand, and on the tray was a boiled egg. Then I thought it was the egg you get the day before you die.

BODIE. What egg is that ?

CINDERELLA (*who in the course of a troubled life has acquired much miscellaneous information*). In the Workhouse you always get an egg to your tea the day before you die. (*She whispers.*) I know now I 'm not the real Cinderella.

BODIE (*taking her hand*). How did you find out ?

CINDERELLA (*gravely*). It 's come to me. The more I eat the clearer I see things. I think it was just an idea of mine ; being lonely-like I needed to have something to hang on to.

BODIE. That was it. Are you sorry you are not the other one ?

CINDERELLA. I 'm glad to be just myself. It 's a pity though about the glass slippers. That 's a lovely idea.

BODIE. Yes.

CINDERELLA. Tell me about *Them.*

BODIE. The children ? They are still with me, of course. I am keeping my promise, and they will be with me till you are able to take care of them again. I have them a great deal in the studio in the day-time.

CINDERELLA (*cogitating*). I wonder if that 's wise.

BODIE. Oh, they don't disturb me much.

CINDERELLA. I was meaning perhaps the smell of the paint would be bad for them.

BODIE. I see! Of course I could give up painting.

CINDERELLA (*innocently*). I think that would be safest.

(MR. BODIE *kicks.*)

Are you kind to Gretchen?

BODIE. I hope so. I feel it 's my duty.

CINDERELLA (*with a sinking*). It 'll not be no use for Gretchen if that 's how you do it. I 'm sure I should get up. (*She attempts to rise.*)

BODIE. Now, now!

CINDERELLA. Are you fond of her, especially when she 's bad?

BODIE (*hurriedly*). Yes, I am, I am! But she is never bad! they are all good, they are like angels.

CINDERELLA (*despairing*). Then they 're cheating you. Where 's my boots?

BODIE. Quiet! That 's all right.

(*A pretty and not very competent* PROBATIONER *comes in at the window, carrying fishing rods, followed by* DANNY *with croquet mallets and balls.*)

PROBATIONER (*laden*). I want to shake hands with you, Mr. Bodie, but you see how I am placed.

CINDERELLA. Do your pretty bow at any rate.

(*The attractive girl does her pretty bow to* MR. BODIE. *It is one of the few things she does well, and will probably by and by bring her into some safe matrimonial harbour; but in her country's great hour she is of less value to it than a ball of twine. She is of a nice nature and would like to be of use, but things slip through her hands as through her mind; she cannot even carry a few lengths of fishing rods without an appeal to heaven. She is counting the pieces now with puckered brow.*)

DANNY (*one of the few men in the world who can carry four croquet balls in two hands*). You see, sir, there is a pond in the garden, and we have a fishing competition; and as there are not enough rods the men hides them so as to be sure of having a rod next day.

PROBATIONER. It is very unfair to the others, Danny.

DANNY (*warmly*). That 's what I say, Nurse.

CINDERELLA. The Matron found a rod the other morning hidden beneath one of the men's mattresses.

PROBATIONER. The odd thing is how he could have got it to the house without being seen. (*Her counting of the pieces ends in her discomfiture.*)

BODIE. Anything wrong?

PROBATIONER. There are only nine pieces. A whole rod is missing!

CINDERELLA (*trembling for her*). Nurse, I 'm so sorry!

BODIE. After all, it 's a trivial matter, isn't it?

PROBATIONER (*her beautiful empty eyes filling*). Trivial! I am responsible. Just think what Dr. Bodie will say to me!

BODIE. Are you afraid of her too?

PROBATIONER. Afraid! I should think I am.

DANNY. And so am I.

(*Before* MR. BODIE *has time to kick, the terrible one reappears.*)

DR. BODIE. I am going over to the Home now, Dick. You must come at once, if you are coming.

BODIE (*cowed and getting his coat*). Yes, all right.

DR. BODIE. A great coat on a day like this! Absurd!

BODIE (*remembering what* CINDERELLA *has told him, and pointing sternly*). French shoes on roads like these, ridiculous!

(DR. BODIE *kicks this time—it is evidently a family trait. Delight of* DANNY.)

DR. BODIE. No. 7, you needn't grin unless there is a reason. Is there a reason?

DANNY. No, no, Doctor.

DR. BODIE. Fishing rods all right this time, Nurse?

PROBATIONER (*faltering*). I am so ashamed, Dr. Bodie; there is one missing.

DR. BODIE. Again. I must ask you, Nurse, to report yourself to the Matron.

PROBATIONER (*crushed*). Yes, Dr. Bodie.

DR. BODIE (*observing that* DANNY *is stealing away unobtrusively*). No. 7.

DANNY (*still backing*). Yes, Doctor.

DR. BODIE. Come here. What is the matter with your right leg; it seems stiff.

DANNY (*with the noble resignation of Tommies, of which he has read in the papers*). It 's a twinge of the old stiffness come back, Doctor. I think there 's a touch of east in the wind. The least touch of east seems to find the hole that bullet made. But I 'm not complaining.

DR. BODIE (*brutally*). No, it is I who am complaining.

(*She feels his leg professionally.*)

Give me that fishing rod.

(*The long-suffering man unbuttons, and to his evident astonishment produces the missing rod.*)

DANNY (*without hope but in character*). Well, I am surprised!

DR. BODIE. You will be more surprised presently. Come along, Dick.

(*She takes her brother away.*)

DANNY (*the magnanimous*). She 's great!

Words couldn't express my admiration for that woman—lady—man—doctor.

PROBATIONER. How mean of you, Danny, to get me into trouble.

DANNY (*in the public school manner*). Sorry. But I 'll have to pay for this. (*Seeing visions.*) She has a way of locking one up in the bathroom.

PROBATIONER (*with spirit*). Let us three conspirators combine to defy her. Carried. Proposed, that No. 7, being a male, conveys our challenge to her. Carried.

CINDERELLA (*gleefully*). Go on, Danny.

DANNY (*of the bull-dog breed*). I never could refuse the ladies. (*He uses the stethoscope as a telephone.*) Give me the Convalescent Home, please. Is that you, Doctor. How are you? We 've just rung up to defy you. Now, now, not another word, or I 'll have you locked up in the bathroom. Wait a mo; there 's a nurse here wants to give you a piece of her mind.

PROBATIONER (*with the stethoscope*). Is that you, Miss Bodie? What? No, I have decided not to call you Dr. Bodie any more.

(*Alas,* DR. BODIE *returns by the window unseen and hears her.*)

Please to report yourself as in disgrace at once to the Matron. That will do. Good-bye. Run along. Heavens, if she had caught us!

DANNY. It would have meant permanent residence in bathroom for me.

(*It is then that they see her.*)

DR. BODIE (*after an awful pause*). I have come back for my stethoscope, Nurse.

(*The* PROBATIONER *can think of no suitable reply.*)

DANNY (*searching his person*). I don't think I have it, Doctor.

DR. BODIE. Don't be a fool, No. 7.

PROBATIONER (*surrendering it*). Here it is, Dr. Bodie, I—I—

DR. BODIE (*charmingly*). Thank you. And, my dear, don't be always Doctor Bodieing me. That, of course, at the Home, and on duty, but here in my house you are my guest. I am Miss Bodie to you here. Don't let me forget that I am a woman. I assure you I value that privilege. (*She lingers over* CINDERELLA'S *pillow*). Dear, you must invite Nurse and Danny to tea with you, and all be happy together. Little Cinderella, if I will do as a substitute, you haven't altogether lost your Godmother.

(*She goes, shaking a reproving finger at* DANNY.)

DANNY. We 're done again!

PROBATIONER (*reduced to tears*). Horrid little toad that I 've been. Some one take me out and shoot me.

(*The* MAID *comes with tea things.*)

DANNY. Allow me, maiden.

ELLEN. Dr. Bodie says I am to bring two more cups.

DANNY (*whose manner is always that of one who, bathroom or no bathroom, feels he is a general favourite*). If you please, child.

PROBATIONER (*as soon as* ELLEN *has gone*). Dr. Bodie is an angel.

DANNY (*quite surprised that he has not thought of this before*). That 's what she is!

CINDERELLA. Danny, can't you say something comforting to poor Nurse,

DANNY (*manfully*). I 'm thankful to say I can. Nurse, I 've often had fits of remorse ; and I can assure you that they soon pass away, leaving not a mark behind.

PROBATIONER. Dear Dr. Bodie !

DANNY. Exactly. You 've taken the words out of my mouth. The only thing for us to think of henceforth is what to do to please her. Her last words to us were to draw up to the tea-table. Are we to disregard the last words of that sublime female ?

PROBATIONER (*recovering*). No !

(*The extra cups having been brought, the company of three settle down to their war-time tea-party, the tray being on* CINDERELLA'S *lap and a guest on each side of her.*)

DANNY. Our plain duty is now to attack the victuals so as to become strong in that Wonder's service. Here 's to dear Dr. Bodie, and may she find plenty to do elsewhere till this party is over.

PROBATIONER (*able to toss her head again*). After all, she put us in a false position.

DANNY. That 's true. Down with her !

PROBATIONER. I drink to you, Danny.

DANNY (*gallantly*). And I reply with mine.

CINDERELLA. It 's queer to think I 'm being—what 's the word ?—hostess.

DANNY. All things are queer ever since the dull old days before the war ; and not the unqueerest is that Daniel Duggan, once a plumber, is now partaking of currant cake with the Lady Charlotte something !

CINDERELLA (*nearly letting her cup fall*). What ?

PROBATIONER. You weren't supposed to know that.

CINDERELLA. Does he mean you ? Are you—?

PROBATIONER. It 's nothing to make a fuss about, Cinderella. How did you find out, Danny ?

DANNY. Excuse me, but your haughty manner of wringing out a dishcloth betrayed you ? My war-worn eyes, of various hues, have had the honour of seeing the Lady Charlotte washing the ward floor. O memorable day ! O glorified floor ! O blushing dishcloth !

PROBATIONER. That was just a beginning. Some day I hope when I rise in the profession to be allowed to wash you, Danny.

DANNY (*bowing grandly*). The pleasure, my lady, will be mutual. (*He hums a tune of the moment.*)

'And when I tell them that some day washed by her I'll be—they'll never believe me'—

PROBATIONER (*with abandon*). 'But when I tell them 'twas a jolly good thing for me—they'll all believe me!'

DANNY. And when I tell them—and I certainly mean to tell them—that one day she'll walk out with me—

(*In a spirit of devilry he crooks his arm; she takes it—she walks out with him for a moment.*)

PROBATIONER (*coming to*). No. 7, what are we doing!

CINDERELLA. It's just the war has mixed things up till we forget how different we are.

PROBATIONER (*with a moment of intuition*). Or

it has straightened things out so that we know how like we are.

(*From the garden comes the sound of a gramophone.*)

CINDERELLA. David 's a long time in coming.

DANNY. The four-twenty 's not in yet.

CINDERELLA. Yes, it is ; I heard the whistle.

DANNY (*sarcastically*). Would you like me to see if he hasn't lost his way ? Those policemen are stupid fellows.

CINDERELLA. None of that, Danny ; but I would like fine if you take a look.

DANNY. Anything to oblige you, though it brings our social to a close. None of these little tea-parties after the war is over, fine lady.

PROBATIONER. Oh dear ! I 'll often enjoy myself less, Danny.

DANNY. Daniel Duggan will sometimes think of this day, when you are in your presentation gown and he is on your roof, looking for that there leakage.

PROBATIONER. Oh, Danny, don't tell me that when I meet you with your bag of tools I 'll be a beast. Surely there will be at least a smile of friendship between us in memory of the old days.

DANNY. I wonder! That's up to you, my lady. (*But he will be wiser if he arranges that it is to be up to himself.*)

PROBATIONER (*calling attention to the music*). Listen! No. 7, to-day is ours.

(*She impulsively offers herself for the waltz; they dance together.*)

DANNY (*when all is over*). Thank you, my lady.

(*She curtsies and he goes out rather finely. It is not likely that her next partner will be equal to her plumber. The two girls are left alone, both nice girls of about the same age; but the poor one has already lived so long that the other, though there may be decades before her, will never make up on* CINDERELLA. *It would be grand to see this waif, the moment after death, setting off stoutly on the next adventure.*)

CINDERELLA. He is a droll character, Danny. (*Examining herself in a hand-mirror.*) Nurse, would you say my hair is looking right? He likes the cap.

PROBATIONER (*who will soon forget her, but is under the spell at present*). Your David ?

CINDERELLA (*on her dignity*). He 's not mine, Nurse.

PROBATIONER. Isn't he ?

CINDERELLA. Hey, hey, hey ! Nurse, when he comes you don't need to stay very long.

PROBATIONER (*in the conspiracy*). I won't.

CINDERELLA (*casually*). He might have things to say to me, you see.

PROBATIONER. Yes, he might.

CINDERELLA (*solemnly*). You and me are both very young, but maybe you understand about men better than I do. You 've seen him, and this is terrible important. Swear by Almighty God you 're to tell me the truth. Would you say that man loves little children ?

PROBATIONER (*touched*). Don't frighten me, Cinderella ; I believe him to be that kind of man. Are you fond of your policeman, dear ?

CINDERELLA (*winking*). That 's telling ! (*Importantly.*) Nurse, did you ever have a love-letter.

PROBATIONER (*gaily*). Not I ! Don't want

to; horrid little explosives! But have you—has he—?

CINDERELLA (*becoming larger*). In my poor opinion, if it 's not a love-letter, it 's a very near thing.

PROBATIONER. If I could see the darling little detestable?

CINDERELLA. Oh no, oh no, no, no, no! But I 'll tell you one thing as is in it. This—'There are thirty-four policemen sitting in this room, but I would rather have you, my dear.' What do you think? That 's a fine bit at the end.

PROBATIONER (*sparkling*). Lovely! Go on, Cinderella, fling reticence to the winds.

CINDERELLA (*doing so*). Unless I am—very far out—in my judgment of men—that man is infatuate about me!

PROBATIONER (*clapping her hands*). The delicious scoundrel! Cinderella, be merciless to him! Knife him, you dear! Give him beans!

CINDERELLA (*gurgling*). I ill-treats him most terrible.

PROBATIONER. That 's the way! down with lovers! slit them to ribbons! stamp on them!

CINDERELLA. Sometimes I— (*She sits up.*) Listen !

PROBATIONER (*alarmed*). It isn't Dr. Bodie, is it ?

CINDERELLA. No, it 's *him.*

PROBATIONER. I don't hear a sound.

CINDERELLA. I can hear him fanning his face with his helmet. He has come in such a hurry. Nurse, you watch me being cruel to him.

PROBATIONER. At him, Cinderella, at him !

DANNY (*flinging open the door*). The Constabulary's carriage stops the way.

(*Our* POLICEMAN *stalks in, wetting his lips as he does so.*)

PROBATIONER (*giving him her hand*). How do you do ? You forget, I dare say, that I met you when you were here last ; but I remember 'our policeman.'

(*He is bashful.*)

There she is.

(*The wicked invalid is looking the other way.*)

POLICEMAN. A visitor to see you, Jane.

CINDERELLA (*without looking round*). I thought it had a visitor's sound. (*She peeps at the* PROBATIONER *gleefully.*)

POLICEMAN (*very wooden*). You don't ask who it is, Jane?

CINDERELLA. I thought it might be that great big ridiculous policeman.

(DANNY *laughs, and our* POLICEMAN *gives him a very stern look.*)

POLICEMAN (*after reflection*). I 'm here again, Jane.

CINDERELLA (*admitting it with a glance*). Perhaps you didn't ought to come so often; it puts them about.

POLICEMAN (*cleverly*). But does it put you about, Jane?

CINDERELLA. Hey! Hey! (*With a cunning waggle of the hand she intimates to the* NURSE *that she may go.*)

DANNY (*who is not so easily got rid of*). You had best be going too, Robert. The lady has answered you in the negative.

POLICEMAN (*lowering*). You make a move there.

(DANNY, *affecting alarm, departs with the* PROBATIONER.)

CINDERELLA. I like fine to hear you ordering the public about, David.

POLICEMAN (*humbly*). I 'm very pleased, Jane, if there 's any little thing about me that gives you satisfaction.

(*He puts down a small parcel that he has brought in.*)

CINDERELLA (*curious*). What 's in the parcel, David ?

POLICEMAN. That remains to be seen. (*He stands staring at his divinity.*)

CINDERELLA (*sneering*). What are you looking at ?

POLICEMAN. Just at you.

CINDERELLA (*in high delight*). Me ? There 's little to look at in me. You should see the larder at the Home. You 'll have a cup of China tea and some of this cake ?

POLICEMAN. No, Jane, no. (*In a somewhat melancholy voice.*) Things to eat have very little interest to me now.

CINDERELLA. Oh ?

POLICEMAN. I 've gone completely off my feed.

(CINDERELLA *would have liked the* PROBATIONER *to hear this.*)

CINDERELLA (*artfully*). I wonder how that can be!

POLICEMAN. Did you get my letter, Jane?

CINDERELLA (*calmly*). I got it—

POLICEMAN. Did you—did you think it was a peculiar sort of a letter?

CINDERELLA (*mercilessly*). I don't mind nothing peculiar in it.

POLICEMAN. There was no word in it that took you aback, was there?

CINDERELLA. Not that I mind of.

POLICEMAN (*worried*). Maybe you didn't read it very careful?

CINDERELLA. I may have missed something. What was the word, David?

POLICEMAN (*in gloom*). Oh, it was just a small affair. It was just a beginning. I thought, if she stands that she 'll stand more. But if you never noticed it— (*He sighs profoundly.*)

CINDERELLA. I 'll take another look—

POLICEMAN (*brightening*). You 've kept it ?

CINDERELLA. I have it here.

POLICEMAN. I could let you see the word if it 's convenient to you to get the letter out of your pocket.

CINDERELLA. It 's not in my pocket.

POLICEMAN. Is it under the pillow ?

CINDERELLA. No.

POLICEMAN (*puzzled*). Where, then ?

(CINDERELLA, *with charming modesty, takes the letter from her bodice. Her lover is thunderstruck.*)

What made you think of keeping it there ?

CINDERELLA. I didn't think, David ; it just came to me.

POLICEMAN (*elate*). It 's infall*ay*ble ! I 'll let you see the word.

CINDERELLA (*smiling at the ridiculous man*). You don't need to bother, David. Fine I know what the word is.

POLICEMAN (*anxious*). And you like it ?

CINDERELLA. If you like it.

POLICEMAN. That emboldens me tremendous.

CINDERELLA. I don't like that so much. If

there 's one thing I like more than any other thing in the world—

POLICEMAN (*eager*). Yes?

CINDERELLA. It 's seeing you, David, tremendous bold before all other folk, and just in a quake before me.

POLICEMAN (*astounded*). It 's what I am. And yet there 's something bold I must say to you.

CINDERELLA (*faltering genteelly*). Is there?

POLICEMAN. It 'll be a staggering surprise to you.

(CINDERELLA *giggles discreetly.*)

I promised the Doctor as I came in not to tire you. (*With some awe.*) She 's a powerful woman that.

CINDERELLA. If you tire me I 'll hold up my hand just like you do to stop the traffic. Go on, David. Just wait a moment. (*She takes off his helmet and holds it to her thin breast.*) Here 's a friend of mine. Now?

POLICEMAN (*despairing of himself*). I wish I was a man in a book. It 's pretty the way they say it; and if ever there was a woman that deserved to have it said pretty to her it 's you. I 've been reading the books. There was one chap that could speak six languages. Jane, I wish I could say it to you in six languages, one down and another come up, till you had to take me in the end.

CINDERELLA. To take you ?

POLICEMAN (*in woe*). Now I 've gone and said it in the poorest, silliest way. Did you hold up your hand to stop me, Jane ?

CINDERELLA. No.

POLICEMAN (*encouraged*). But I 've said it. Will you, Jane ?

CINDERELLA (*doggedly*). Will I what ?

POLICEMAN. Do you not see what I 'm driving at ?

CINDERELLA. Fine I see what you 're driving at.

POLICEMAN. Then won't you help me out ?

CINDERELLA. No.

POLICEMAN. If you could just give me a shove.

CINDERELLA (*sympathetically*). Try Badgery.

POLICEMAN (*brightening*). Have you forgotten that pool in Badgery Water where the half-pounder used— No, you never was there! Jane, the heart of me is crying out to walk with you by Badgery Water.

CINDERELLA. That 's better!

POLICEMAN. I would never think of comparing Mrs. Bodie to you. For my part I think nothing of uppers. Feet for me.

(*She gives him her hand to hold.*)

My dear.

CINDERELLA. You said *that* was only a beginning.

POLICEMAN. My dearest.

CINDERELLA (*glistening*). I 'm not feeling none tired, David.

POLICEMAN. My pretty.

CINDERELLA. Hey! Hey! Hey! Hey!

POLICEMAN. I don't set up to be a prince, Jane; but I love you in a princely way, and if you would marry me, you wonder, I 'll be a true man to you till death us do part. Come on, Cinders. (*Pause.*) It 's the only chance that belt of mine has.

CINDERELLA. No, no, I haven't took you

yet. There 's a thing you could do for me, that would gratify me tremendous.

POLICEMAN. It 's done.

CINDERELLA. I want you to let me have the satisfaction, David, of having refused you once.

POLICEMAN. Willingly ; but what for ?

CINDERELLA. I couldn't say. Just because I 'm a woman. Mind you, I dare say I 'll cast it up at you in the future.

POLICEMAN. I 'll risk that. Will you be my princess, Jane ?

CINDERELLA. You promise to ask again ? At once ?

POLICEMAN. Yes.

CINDERELLA. Say—I do.

POLICEMAN. I do.

CINDERELLA (*firmly*). It 's a honour you do me, policeman, to which I am not distasteful. But I don't care for you in that way, so let there be no more on the subject. (*Anxiously.*) Quick, David !

POLICEMAN. For the second time, will you marry me, Jane ?

CINDERELLA (*who has been thinking out the*

answer for several days). David, I love thee, even as the stars shining on the parched earth, even as the flowers opening their petals to the sun; even as mighty ocean with its billows; even so do I love thee, David. (*She nestles her head on his shoulder.*)

POLICEMAN. If only I could have said it like that!

CINDERELLA (*happily*). That 's just a bit I was keeping handy. (*Almost in a whisper.*) David, do you think I could have a engagement ring?

POLICEMAN (*squaring his shoulders*). As to that, Jane, first tell me frankly, do you think the Police Force is romantical?

CINDERELLA. They 're brave and strong, but—

POLICEMAN. The general verdict is no. And yet a more romantical body of men do not exist. I have been brooding over this question of engagement rings, and I consider them unromantical affairs. (*He walks toward his parcel.*)

CINDERELLA. David, what 's in that parcel?

POLICEMAN. Humbly hoping you would have

me, Jane, I have had something special made for you—

CINDERELLA (*thrilling*). Oh, David, what is it?

POLICEMAN. It 's a policeman's idea of an engagement ring—

CINDERELLA. Quick ! Quick !

POLICEMAN. —for my amazing romantical mind said to me that, instead of popping a ring on the finger of his dear, a true lover should pop a pair of glass slippers upon her darling feet.

CINDERELLA. David, you 're a poet !

POLICEMAN (*not denying it*). It 's what you 've made me—and proud I would be if, for the honour of the Force, I set this new fashion in engagement rings. (*He reveals the glass slippers.*)

(CINDERELLA *holds out her hands for the little doves.*)

They 're not for hands. (*He uncovers her feet.*)

CINDERELLA. They 're terrible small ! Maybe they 'll not go on !

(*They go on.*)

CINDERELLA. They 're like two kisses.

POLICEMAN. More like two love-letters.

CINDERELLA. No, David, no,—kisses.

POLICEMAN. We won't quarrel about it, Cinders; but at the same time. . . . However!

(*He presses her face to him for a moment so that he may not see its transparency.* DR. BODIE *has told him something.*)